FORTY YEARS *of* FOOD

FORTY YEARS *of* FOOD

KIM CAIN

For information about special discounts for bulk purchases, please contact Trilogy Christian Publishing.

Manufactured in the United States of America

10 9 8 7 6 5 4 3 2 1

Library of Congress Cataloging-in-Publication Data is available.

ISBN 978-1-64088-197-6

ISBN 978-1-64088-198-3 (ebook)

Dedication

For my daughter, Melinda; my granddaughters, Karsyn, and Alexis. For all the daughters. You are perfect just the way you are.

Foreword

One simple sentence was all it took: "Hey, Margaret, come sit here with us." Kim extended that invitation to me early on in our sixth-grade year (sometime in early '70s) in the school cafeteria. Being a shy, pimply, awkward pre-teen and feeling lost, I anxiously and gratefully took her up on her offer. That kind gesture was the start of a friendship that has spanned over four decades and still counting. I've joked with Kim often saying she invited me to sit down one time, and I just never left.

We've shared many laughs and heartaches, smiles and tears. I was absolutely devastated when she had to move away due to her parents' divorce. Changes happen in life, but though them all and despite the many miles between us, our friendship never waned. Kim had been living in New Jersey when my mother passed away in 1993. She had called my mother's house that day to get my current phone number and was given the news. After having worked all day, she made the two hour drive to Long Island, just to be there for me and had to drive back that same night.

I remember vividly many of the stories she recounts in her book. I remember her being hospitalized while we were in high school. I went to visit her during her stay. I remember the craziness that surrounded her parents' divorce. I remember her older sister always trying to catch us doing something wrong to get Kim in trouble.

What I didn't know was all that Kim was dealing with behind the scenes—on her own. I had no idea until she shared her book with me. I was stunned! Back in our junior & senior high school days, we spoke of dieting and our wanting to lose weight a lot. We were like many teenaged girls with a poor body image. We wanted to fit in and worried (or obsessed) our looks weren't good enough. We even joined a gym together. However, I had no idea Kim had started to take things to an extreme extent. Nor did I know that she spent much of her life trying to battle and conquer a treacherous eating disorder. How scary it must have been for her!

Others who have suffered from and endured this debilitating disease, or still do, will relate to much, if not all, of Kim's story. The feelings of isolation, desperation, and shame are common, no doubt. May these dear souls find some solace and relief in knowing they are NOT alone. May they also find the fortitude to keep their fight going, gather support from their loved ones, and seek help. If the reader, like me, is unfamiliar with bulimia, Kim's book, *Forty Years of Food*, sheds light on a topic of which I had little understanding. She opens a window to let us get a glimpse of what life is like for a food addict, each day filled with struggle and a gamut of emotions.

With candor and great wit, Kim has let us into her world, that until now, has remained secret. She gives us her first-hand account boldly with straightforward honesty. A story that is both compelling and heartbreaking but also filled with the hope and knowledge of God's love. Kim's faith is unwavering.

I admire Kim for her bravery in writing this book. It is courageous of her to put herself out there not only for the world to see but especially her family. Prior to her writing this book, they, too, were unaware.

This book is one of the many reasons I admire Kim. I am certainly proud to call her my oldest and dearest friend. I am forever blessed and grateful that she uttered that one simple sentence, way back when, "Hey, Margaret, come sit here with us." We're still counting the decades.

—Peggy Callaghan Ingram
(Margaret)

Acknowledgments

A heart felt Thank you….

To Mark Mingle, my Agent, for his genuine love of my book and confidence that it needed to be published! I wasn't expecting such an encouraging reaction! His inspiration was contagious and love of Christ evident.

To the editor at Trilogy Publishing, Jim Miller, for making me sound literate.

For my Mom, My Hero. I hope you are proud of me. I miss you terribly. I am trying to "Be Strong".

For My husband Bill, who has admitted to reading only three books in his entire life, one of them mine! For his continued love and support of my complicated disease and his desire to see me get well.

For My oldest and dearest friend Peg Callaghan Ingram, a lifetime childhood friend from the 6th grade, whose courage and lifestyle have inspired my words. Her presence can be felt in all my childhood stories.

For my friend Patty Donlon, whom I met in my early OA days, attending meetings together, working the program together, and trying to get well together. We have remained friends and confidantes throughout our turbulent years of food addiction. She "gets" me, my disease, and my daily struggle with food.

For My grandchildren, Karsyn, Bryson, Alexis, Mason, Jordan, Logan & Landon, who motivate me to want to live a long life. Who ARE my life. Grammie loves you to the moon and back.

Mostly, for My God whose word inspires me every day and whose *voice* directed me to write this book!

Illustrations to be found on pages 59-72

Introduction

Last year while driving home on the freeway, God told me to write a book. He even gave me the title! However, it was a book about procrastination, and I never wrote it. No, I'm not trying to be funny. Although I spent months working on it, I only managed to write two pages! No words would come. But His urging continued, and I listened.

I'm not sure how this book will be different, but it's not about procrastination, and it is my life story, a subject I am very familiar with. And it is an important book that I believe needs to be written: words that need to be read, hurts that need to be healed, for lives that need to be changed. I am praying for the courage to share my story with my family and my friends, as I secretly struggle with an eating disorder and food addiction even today as I write these words. The adverse effect it has had on our lives throughout the years, without them even being aware, is profound. I pray for their understanding and forgiveness as I spend the latter part of my life in utter resignation that I may never be healed from this dreadful disease. But also in appreciation that God can use broken people for his divine purpose. He uses our trials to humble us, to gain our attention, and to teach us his ways. This book is dedicated to the millions of young girls, women, and even grandmothers, like myself, who have suffered or continue to suffer miserably; to those with shattered lives who place their value by a number on a scale: a generation void of self-esteem, self-love, and self-respect. I hope this book helps those who are beginning a lifetime journey with food. May God be with you as you struggle trying to have the perfect body that society so unfairly requires. May you find the peace you deserve and so badly desire. I am still searching.

Table of Contents

Prologue

I loved Fridays at school during my elementary school days! It was Pizza Day for lunch. I would stand in line and wait patiently for my pizza tray, always asking for an extra cheese stick. I loved those cheese sticks that were placed, like perfection, on top of the square pizza slice. I can still see it in my mind; a three-inch rectangle of orange cheddar cheese that could be picked up and consumed before the first bite of greasy pizza. It still brings me joy thinking about it! I recall walking my empty tray to the counter at the end of lunch period and being astonished that some of my peers had left their cheese sticks, discarded, on the side of their tray, forgotten, uneaten! How could they resist that mouthwatering block of cheese? I often considered quickly grabbing a piece of uneaten cheese from their dirty tray and eating it, but didn't, in fear someone would see me. In retrospect, that's an odd thought for a young child. Most kids were busy thinking of more important things in grade school, like friends and playtime activities. I stood lingering over the cafeteria garbage can lusting after discarded cheese.

Chapter 1

The Beginning of the End

The first time I realized I was fat I was in second grade. I was absent from school the day my class was scheduled for their annual physical exam, which in 1970 was performed in the school nurse's office. The basic information: height, weight, eye examination, hearing test, vaccination records, were recorded on a small white card and brought back to the classroom to be presented to the teacher. Upon returning to school the next day, I was promptly sent down the hall for a make-up exam. I remember stepping on to the enormous metal scale and looking up at the number. I'm not sure how I knew that number was too high. I'm sure I didn't know what it should be. I was seven years old!

I studied the handwritten numbers on that little folded card all the way back to the classroom. Decades later, I'm still confused as to why I had to bring the card back to my teacher. It seems like that information should have stayed in the nurse's office. I didn't want to give it to her, and I vaguely remember being nervous while handing it to her quickly. With apprehension, I hurried back to my seat, hoping she wouldn't bother to look at it. However, and this is life changing, before I could sit down I heard her say out loud, "Wow, sixty-five pounds, chubby little girl." I remember those words precisely so many years later.

Now I am sure my teacher, an older woman in her sixties at the time, did not intentionally want to hurt me or could ever know the trigger that those words set off in me. After all, it was the early Seventies; eating disorders were just beginning to gain attention. Many at the time would not have been familiar with this new disease raging in teen girls and woman all over the world. Not until many years later did we realize the significance and assign specific names for these diseases, anorexia and bulimia. Names that I would, unfortunately, become all too familiar with my entire life. Bulimia is a disease I am still struggling with today and a battle I am losing very badly.

I remember, precisely after that day, I developed an unusual awareness of my weight. I thought about food often and enjoyed eating way too much, not realizing at the time the emotional bond that was beginning to develop. Even at this young age, I was increasingly becoming obsessed with food and with my appearance. It may have been a genetic trigger or possibly a learned behavior that created my food obsession and poor self-image. I understand now that it had been subconsciously instilled in me at an early age that thin was attractive and beautiful, and fat was bad and ugly.

My mom and my sister were overweight and often on diets, happy and optimistic as they lost unwanted pounds, and soon after, despondent and discouraged as they gained it all back. Ironically, growing up, I was always the skinny one! At sixty-five pounds—and yes, I remember that number vividly—it was hardly off the charts! I can only compare it now to my granddaughter who just turned seven and is currently in second grade. She weighed in at a whopping fifty-nine pounds this year! (One of the reasons this book is so important!) And she is super skinny! I call her Bones. So, I don't believe I was overweight, or remotely fat, probably just larger proportioned with a heavy frame. Still, for some reason, that number on the card clearly jumped out at my teacher! She innocently commented on what she saw and perceived to be too high of a number. My lifetime journey of poor body image began, and thus my lifetime of food addiction and bulimia.

I am aware that one comment from my second-grade teacher was not the cause of my eating disorder. I absolutely believe I was predestined to spend my life struggling with food. I refuse to blame anyone. I am responsible for myself, for my own actions and for the course I have chosen for my life. However, there were determining factors that I believe led to my lifetime battle with food that may help others with signals to watch for in themselves and their families.

My eating disorder, bulimia nervosa, physically began at the age of fourteen and was brought on by many events in my life. I was born and raised on Long Island with my parents and older sister. My first home was an apartment directly upstairs from a candy store/laundromat. This was very convenient for Mom and a dream come true for kids! She would send my older sister and I downstairs with a few pennies, and we would come back with a bag full of treats! This became a daily routine. We certainly enjoyed perks while living there, and it seemed perfectly normal to eat bags of candy every day! I'm not sure if my first few years of life eating large amounts of sugar led to my struggle with food. Mercifully, a few years later our family purchased and moved into a three-bedroom house where I spent my childhood school years right up until high school, with the nearest candy store a good mile away!

My dad worked at Grumman, a huge aerospace corporation that amazingly built the Lunar Excursion Module (LEM) for the first moon landing in 1969! I remembered that he loved his job, and was very proud of himself. He worked long hours and made a good living. My mom worked the swing shift as a caregiver at a local hospital where she took care of elderly patients. He was Catholic, and she was Jewish. Raised Catholic, I also had the blessing of experiencing and later falling in love with my Jewish heritage. Although I wouldn't truly appreciate it until much later in life as I read daily through the words of the Bible, especially the Jewish history of the Old Testament.

I was a young adult when I surrendered my life to Christ. Becoming a Christian was the direct result of having an eating disorder as I will go into later. Through a lifetime of pain and brokenness, I have been blessed by a relationship with Jesus Christ. He has sustained me over the years with my ongoing, daily struggle with this disease. This book is not about God; it's about my life long addiction to food and bulimia nervosa that continues now, well into my adulthood. Even as a Grandmother I continue to fight with the guilt of a disease that has ravaged my life. I must give credit where credit is due. It is only by the grace of Jesus Christ, and Him alone, that I have the ability and ongoing desire to write this book. He unmistakably has a plan to use me in a way that will help others. It is through my failures that I have become humble and broken enough to seek God's help. If I could have managed on my own, I would have no need for God. This life failure was the opportunity to start again. As Christians we are called to love and serve others, and amidst a raging disease I am being obedient and allowing God to use me. He can clearly use shattered lives to bring healing to others.

Chapter 2

1970-something

Recalling my childhood, I recognize now that many of my memories were about food! I'm sure it's not a coincidence, and I can appreciate that my obsession with food was probably always there. My second-grade teacher's comment just reinforced what I had felt prior to that day on the scale.

Perhaps it all began at the age of two, when as my extremely tired, working mom tried to sleep, my older sister fed me a jar of cream deodorant, evidently popular back in 1965, I happily consumed the entire jar. The result was a trip to the emergency room to have my stomach pumped. My sister, to this day, will tell this story with pride in her voice. As if almost killing your baby sister was the greatest achievement of her life!

A year or so later, again with a tired mom and big sister safely off to school, I was left on my own. I sat eating an enormous bowl of cereal that I managed to pour for myself. I positioned it on a fold out table set at the end of sleepy Mother's bed, then dutifully knocked over the entire tray. Milk and cereal spewed all over the bed. With Mom wet and screaming, I never missed a spoonful or a beat of Tom & Jerry on our 13-inch, black-and-white TV. I remember trying desperately to finish eating the now-almost-empty bowl as my Mother jumped up and started to clean my mess.

Shortly after that, I managed to get a large chunk of hard, sticky candy stuck in the backseat ashtray—yes, ashtray—of my dad's brand-new, red 1968 Chevy Impala. After I was specifically warned never to eat anything in Daddy's new car! My dad had a wicked temper (one of the family secrets).

It took him 30 minutes, and a good deal of cussing, to get the candy unstuck and the ashtray clean again. That piece of candy got me in big trouble. My desire for sugar was becoming problematic.

Our little family used to travel to Brooklyn twice a month to visit my grandparents in Sheepshead Bay. It was about an hour's drive from our Long Island home. They lived in a three-story brownstone on Ave X, right next to the Jewish Temple where they attended services regularly. I used to watch the people come in and out of the synagogue, the men with little black caps on their heads, some with long beards. Nothing like I had ever witnessed living on Long Island in a generally exclusive Catholic area. All my friends and I attended Catechism together on Sundays. Our mothers would car pool us back and forth to save gas, which in the Seventies, during odd and even fill up days, could be a sought-after commodity. Indeed, we all received our sacrament of Communion together that same spring.

The highlight of those Brooklyn trips, almost as exciting as crossing over the drawbridge on the Belt Parkway, were the bagels we would stop and get on the Ave before heading home (not readily available on the Island at the time). A Bakers Dozen! Which in layman's terms is thirteen bagels for the price of twelve. At that time, my friends in the neighborhood didn't even know what a bagel was. I found that amazing. I remember eating them hot, straight out of the bag, all the way home, not even holding out for a little shmear of cream cheese when we arrived home, a habit I have kept to this day when I buy fresh bagels from the bakery.

Another time, my dad had cooked up a box of Lipton chicken soup for my lunch, made with extra pastina noodles, of course! It was my favorite soup. I had the habit of doing weird stuff with my food and always added cold milk to my hot soup prior to eating it. I quickly finished the entire bowl then demanded that he pour the remainder of what was in the pot into my bowl, which he did. I enthusiastically finished it up. What I didn't see until I was done was Dad's empty bowl and spoon sitting on the counter next to the stove. He was going to have some soup too! Never considering that he also could be hungry, I greedily wanted every drop. My obsession was in full swing already.

It was a profound moment for a little child. I have thought about this moment many times over the years, and it has always made me feel sad. Not because he missed lunch, but that the fact that he also could be hungry never entered my mind. It was always about me. Self-centeredness would become a lifetime trait that I despised in myself. As I got older and more mature, I would constantly have to make conscious efforts to take the focus off myself and concentrate on others' needs. I was also learning that food gave me only a temporary high, and invariably I would eat too much and end up feeling worse than before I started!

I loved Fridays at school during my elementary school days. It was Pizza Day for lunch! I would stand in line and wait patiently for my pizza tray, always asking for an extra cheese stick. I loved those cheese sticks that were placed, like perfection, on top of the square pizza slice. I can still see it in my mind: a three-inch rectangle of orange cheddar cheese that could be picked up and consumed before the first bite of greasy pizza. It still brings me joy thinking about it! I recall walking my empty tray to the counter at the end of lunch period and being astonished that some of my peers had left their cheese sticks, discarded, on the side of their tray, forgotten, uneaten! How could they resist that mouthwatering block of cheese? I often considered quickly grabbing a piece of uneaten cheese from their dirty tray and eating it, but I didn't, in fear someone would see me. In retrospect, that's an odd thought for a young child. Most kids were busy thinking of more important things in grade school, like friends and playtime activities. I stood lingering over the cafeteria garbage can lusting after discarded cheese.

The summer I turned eight, I had the opportunity to go to day summer camp at the local beach for a few weeks. We spent the day happily swimming, painting and crafting. My fondest memory of those camp days was the bagged lunch we received! Every day at lunchtime, brown paper sack lunches were distributed between the children. This was the highlight of my day that I looked forward to upon arriving in the morning! I clearly remember the thrill of ripping the bag open at lunchtime to see my surprise sandwich. It could be tuna, one of my favorites, or ham with mustard and mayo, or an occasional peanut butter and strawberry jam on wheat, which I adore to this day. I would also bargain with my camp friends for their leftover food in trade of crafts I had made. I often gathered the uneaten leftovers to bring home at the end of the day and hide in my room where I would finish them up that night in secret. At eight years old, I was already hoarding and hiding food, another lifetime habit that continues with me to this very day.

Like most kids, I would come home from school famished. Once in the door I immediately raced to the freezer to find one of my favorite after-school snacks, a frozen beef and gravy meal in a bag! It was the Seventies and frozen TV dinners were extremely popular. Simply set the frozen meat bag in a pot of boiling water, (pre-microwave days), cook for five minutes, and pour it over two slices of white bread. It's no wonder as an adult I chose to become a vegetarian! It was hardly a snack and more of a meal, which wouldn't have been too bad, except that I would eat three or four of them at a time! Then, in panic, I'd try to rearrange the freezer afterwards so my mom wouldn't notice they were all gone. I'm not sure if my mom did ever notice missing food during this time. Mercifully, there was a great deal going on in her life with her marital problems, and missing food probably wasn't something on her mind. Although, I do recollect her saying quite frequently, "I thought I just went shopping.... Did you guys eat it up already?" I would often throw my older sister under the bus for the food I had eaten.

I can recall sleeping over at a friend's house, and she had to ask her mom if we could have a snack. She had to ask first? This was foreign to me as my sister and I (except when she wasn't dieting with Mom) had free reign of the food in the house! Snack after snack, without asking, and it seemed normal to me! In retrospect, I wouldn't allow my own grandchildren to have access to unlimited junk. Although, as a grandmother, I am allowed a little wiggle room! However, there are limits. I grew up with very few limits. There were no boundaries as far as food was concerned and no knowledge of when enough is enough.

Regrettably, I raised my own children this way, not fully realizing the damage I was causing until I was older and mature, with a little wisdom under my belt. The saying, "With age comes wisdom," is certainly true, as only an older person can fully understand. Yes, we make mistakes, but they are made with much more thought and consideration than back in our younger, foolish years, which for me, were my 20s and early 30s, and sometimes still now at the age of 55! I wish I could have known then what I know now, even in my active disease. Although, I have learned that struggle and difficult situations bring us to a more intimate relationship with God.

One afternoon I was playing outside with my friends, wearing a pair of stretchy blue paisley shorts that made me feel fat. I was about nine years old, and I hated those shorts! They were polyester with an elastic waistband, and I was always tugging on them and fixing them while I had them on. I hadn't really developed a sense of style yet, and I was quite content just wearing the clothes my mom bought for me. However, something about these shorts have always stuck in my mind:

the fact that I hated wearing them! I despised how they looked on me. I remembered the scene where I am playing in the street in front of my house with my friends, taking a time out from our game, and running in to change my clothes for no reason other than I felt fat. (Felt fat at nine years old?) The beginning of my lifetime of poor body image.

Chapter 3

Food Memories

Amazingly, beyond the food memories, initially, I only have vague recollections from my childhood. This may be a blessing. A few years ago, if you asked me if I had a good childhood, I would probably say something like, "It was fine, perfectly normal!"

I would have said that I had a typical childhood from the Seventies. It was a slower, easier time. Pre-techy stage, no cell phones, computers, iPads; things that today's kids cannot imagine living without. But we did! We went outside to run around and played with our friends all day and part of the night, until it got dark and the street lamps came on, or your mom flicked the porch light on and off. Worse than that, she screamed your name at the top of her lungs to come home! We did! Exhausted, dirty, and ready for a snack.

I was always ready for a snack! I loved to eat. I still do. Again, I was never an overweight child, I was Skinny Minnie, like my dad. But the obsession was there. The poor self-image was there. I remember my mom and sister attempted several different diets throughout the years. Although I was not dieting, I felt deprived too because we couldn't keep any good food in the house during those times. I would often walk to the corner store and buy full size candy bars for eight cents each. I would eat all four Snickers bars (still my favorite, and since then available in King size!) before I returned home because I couldn't bring them into the house, and truthfully, because I couldn't stop eating them until they were gone. I realize now that my addiction to sugar was also developing. Additionally, there was a great deal going on in my life that ultimately fed my addiction. I used food to calm me down, to cheer me up, and to avoid facing problems. Years later I realized that excess food would let me down rather than solve my problems, and an abundance of food increased them. Rather than solving my problems, overeating had multiplied them. I pretended everything was fine for so long that I believed it. As a child I was are unable to recognize and express distress; I buried it. Even as an adult I never knew what I was really feeling. I would get high on food, chewing my emotions away.

Halloween time as a kid was truly a wonderful time for me. My mom would dress me in a plastic costume with a matching rubber-band mask. I would set out into the neighborhood with a pillow case (my bag for the candy collected) and flour sack (you will only get this if you are a baby boomer), and off I would go on a mission to "hit" (go to) every house in my neighborhood. I had a precise plan to go up and down each and every one of the dozen or so blocks in my neighborhood, which I considered my territory. I went up one side of the street, methodically going to each house, then back down the same block hitting all the houses on the way back. The "weaving back and forth method" I tried the previous year, turned out to be less effective, it took more time, and I could miss a house! Going up one side of the street and back down the other was a good system that, twelve blocks later, yielded quite a bit of candy.

I would eat a good portion of the candy as I was out, depositing the wrappers back into my pillowcase. To my horror as I emptied my huge sack onto my bed at home, I realized how much I had eaten already. Then I meticulously went through all the candy and sorted into three piles: good candy, acceptable candy, and desperate candy only to be eaten once everything else was gone. I was stingy with my candy, not wanting to share with anyone, often hiding my lot for several weeks. I would also steal my sister's candy and put it into my stash when I could. I had it down to a science and would often have candy left straight through to Christmas.

During this time there was heavy construction going on in our community. The road directly in front of our home was torn up and closed during this time. We had to park at the corner of the street and walk to our house for about a month or so. The construction workers in those holes were thirsty and being entrepreneurs, my friends and I decided to sell ice-cold iced tea each day. We made a small fortune intending to save most of it for NY Mets tickets, and T-Shirts with matching iron-on names. However, I couldn't save my money, often spending it on candy and treats from the ice cream truck. Mr. Softee was a favorite of mine, although any ice cream truck would do. I would run blocks to catch him waving my dollar bill in the air and screaming, "Stop" at the top of my lungs! He did, after driving a little too long before "seeing" me and watching me run desperately behind him.

My mom bailed me out in the end, giving me the money I needed to go see the Mets at Shea Stadium with my friends. It's a habit that was tough to break as I got older. Seeking instant gratification and not thinking or planning for the future. It's a tough lesson that ultimately needs to be learned, sometimes the hard way. Sin does have consequences. We are all ultimately responsible for ourselves and our actions.

One Spring during the school year, my grandmother, who lived directly across the street, made a bag lunch for my sister and I every day. This allowed us to save our lunch money for a "Mother's ring" we were buying as a surprise for our mom.

Each day on the way to the bus stop, my sister and I would stop at Nanny's house and drop off our lunch money (50 cents each). In exchange we received a bag lunch made by Nanny. We did this faithfully for a month until we had enough money to purchase the Mother's Day ring. I always convinced my

Nanny that I didn't get enough food. She would often sneak extra snacks in my lunch bag, unbeknownst to my sister who would have had a fit.

I have this lovely ring now after my mom's death in 2012. It is one of my most cherished possessions that I wear on a chain around my neck often.

Christmas time at Nanny's house was something I always looked forward to because of the homemade chocolate chip cookies Nanny used to bake. A month before Christmas day she would start baking, from scratch, filling large Tupperware bowls with these delectable cookies! I would stop by daily and indulge in as many cookies as I could get away with eating. At the time I didn't realize I was actually binging on them, stuffing them into my mouth without thinking, wrapping a few in paper napkins to bring home for later. I can still taste them in my mind today. They were by far the best cookies I have ever eaten in my life. My Nanny has been gone many years now. I wonder if she thought it odd that I could eat so many at one time. She never said anything to me. She may have wondered how I could eat so much, but the joy of watching her granddaughter delight and enjoy her cookies probably far outweighed any comment she wanted to make.

Chapter 4

It's Not Always What it Seems

I didn't realize this until a lifetime later, after witnessing first hand my father's verbal abuse towards my mother. Long after they retired, when she was very sick and became totally dependent on him, the memories came flooding back. Before this time, it had never occurred to me that we didn't have a normal, happy childhood. Up to this point in my adult life I didn't have any memories of my childhood. I always assumed, except for my parent's divorce and remarriage, that it was a normal childhood. Looking back, there must have been some reason for the divorce!

My sister and I were kept away from the details at the time. I know my dad was addicted to Valium for a short time. They were being incorrectly prescribed like candy back in the day. We were told to hide all the knives in the house, but we didn't know why. He went through a full-blown withdrawal, and at the time, I didn't fully understand what was happening. He took some time off work to recover. I remember him walking around the kitchen table day and night. For hours on end, he walked around our little four-chair dining room table set. Again, I didn't know why at the time. No one explained to me what was happening. Much later I realized that is how he survived getting through his drug withdrawal cold turkey!

It was a very confusing time for me. My mother had left and was no longer living with us. She may have been involved with someone else. We were all unquestionably terrified of my dad.

His bouts of anger could be fierce. It was many years later, when my parents had retired and my father was taking care of my ailing mother that the floodgates opened. I started to have memories of this time from my childhood. My mother would say things to me on the phone, but not plainly. It was like she wanted to tell me something but couldn't. She would call to say hello, but wouldn't talk, just kept me on the line for a while saying nothing. I would ask if everything was okay, and she always assured me it was. I would later call my dad to check on her, and he would assure me everything was okay.

They lived five hours away, and I couldn't see what was going on daily, only what I could see during our visits. I found out several years later from my mother right before her death that he was verbally (possibly physically?) abusive to her. She was dependent on him and needed constant care the last five years of her life. She was afraid to rock the boat in fear of being alone. I would have taken care of her! I didn't know. Although my instincts were screaming at the time, because of my active addiction, I couldn't read my emotions very well.

My father went so far as to physically leave her, renting an apartment an hour away without telling my sister or myself! My extremely sick mother was left alone! She never mentioned it at the time, I believe out of fear of him. I'm not sure how long he was gone. He eventually returned, apparently not too long later, out of his guilt that he couldn't live with. The fact that he went so far as to rent an apartment, furnish it, and physically move leads me to believe that things were not good for either one of them. But it must have been far worse for my mother who needed him to physically care for her and suffered from his verbal abuse. The memories of his abuse and details of events of her later years of life with him, only came into realization after she passed away. The childhood memories came back, causing the repressed feelings to surface in full force, compelling me to evaluate my raw emotions. Repressed emotions that I have been eating over my entire life.

My dad had a nasty temper. Back in the day, the phone was attached directly to the wall. The phone company would come in and hardwire it when you ordered phone service. You couldn't move it or change to another outlet. It was installed to that spot on the wall permanently. Unless you were my dad, and you received the phone bill in the mail that was too high. Then you would violently rip the phone off the wall and throw it across the room! My dad had done this on more than one occasion. I distinctly remember my mother talking to the phone technician a few days later as he was repairing and reinstalling the phone line. Trying to hide the fact that the phone had been torn from the wall when clearly that's what had happened, she did her best to hide her embarrassment and cover for him. To my mother's relief, the technician politely reinstalled the line to the wall and never said a word.

On another occasion, in a surge of anger (I can't recall the exact details of why my dad was angry), I remember him lifting our 26-inch TV, which was pretty big back in the day, off of its rolling stand and throwing it across the room. It hit a wall, smashing it to bits and leaving a large hole. It came very close to hitting my sister and the dog. We all ran. Luckily, Dad was very handy and could fix almost anything, especially walls (but not phone lines or TVs). We had to buy a new one the very next day. He was always very sorry the next day, and we reaped the good rewards of his guilt, but we knew it was temporary.

My mom worked the swing shift at the hospital and on a few occasions, arrived home after midnight to find one of her beloved pets out in the cold. That night, my sister and I were bad, and as a punishment we had to put our dog, whom we adored, outside in the snow. She had to be outside our front gate, and completely off the property. My dad was a very good punisher, and really hit where it hurt. Besides the snow, it was a very cold night in the teens. Sobbing, we did what we were told, but not before dressing her in a sweater with attempts to put socks on all her feet. We were told to look at her outside the front gate, staring at us in confusion, in the cold one last time before we were sent to bed. We cried ourselves to sleep knowing in the morning we would find her frozen and dead. My mom, of course, rescued her on the way in from work that night, and she was happily wagging her tail and greeting us that morning.

Another time, again as a punishment to us, he made us put our indoor cat outside in the detached garage. "Lucky" was scared, never having even been outside before. We tried to put food and water out, but Dad wouldn't let us. We were sure he would starve and freeze to death by the morning. We could hear him howling from our upstairs bedroom window until mercifully, we cried ourselves to sleep. Upon arriving home from work, my mother attempted to rescue him, but the terrified cat climbed up into the rafters and wouldn't come down. He stayed there all night until the morning when, before leaving for work, my dad had to get a ladder and pull him down, getting scratched up badly during the process. I remember thinking that he deserved it, and I was happy the cat got back at him. My sister and I secretly laughed at him when we saw his arms bleeding from the scratches.

There have been a few extremely malicious memories that have played back many times over the years. I was nine years old, and because of the many sugary foods I would eat, I was also obsessed with brushing my teeth. This obsession has remained with me over the years, although I have let up slightly as I got older. I would brush my teeth ten times a day as a kid if I could get away with it but always at night before bed. I had a 20-minute ritual of cleaning every tooth individually with the tip of the tooth brush. It didn't help that I had an aunt who was a dental tech who once showed me a huge set of fake teeth, opened them up, and showed me how to properly clean each one! Putting the fear of God in me that if I didn't clean them three times a day they could all fall out! I literally could not sleep if I didn't brush my teeth. My older sister will vouch for this as I used to drive her crazy with my ritual.One night, while my mother worked, my sister and I were sent to bed early by Dad because we were bad. I decided to sneak out of bed into my bathroom quickly to brush my teeth. I could do this fast if I had to. But I was caught! Again, my dad was a brilliant punisher, and always creative, making sure we remembered how bad we were. He told me get my brand-new Girl Scout Workbook that I needed for my very first girl scout meeting the next day. I was a new girl scout and was extremely excited to attend my first meeting with my starched green uniform and new book! I anxiously gave it to him. He tossed it into the burning fireplace! It must have been cold outside, although I don't specifically remember the weather. I do remember the flames. I was told to sit there and watch it burn. He had been very clear about that. I remember he repeated it several times, "Watch it burn." In his attempt to really hurt me, he wouldn't let me look away. It worked. In complete despair, I did just that, quietly weeping in fear of more trouble.

A few minutes later, my sister's new book was added to the burning flames, her penance for laughing at me. We both sat in front of the raging fire and silently cried until the flames completely burned out the last pages of the books. Then he forced us to continue to watch the ashes before sending us to bed. I was grateful that I had at least brushed my teeth and could finally fall sleep. My mom bought us both new books the next day. She was always softening our blows from Dad. I didn't see it then but realize now how much this must have hurt her, trying to protect us.

And now, the grand finale of memories. Not the last, but the most disturbing memory for me as a child, which only came into my recollection many years later as an adult. It is difficult to think about to this day and equally as embarrassing to write about. I am sharing this for the sole purpose of revealing the extreme extent of his control and anger towards us and the ultimate effect it has had on my life as a food addict. It happened when I was five years old, in my dad's new, red Chevy 1968 Impala, which he loved.

Driving home on a weekend trip from Brooklyn, which at the time would have taken us a good hour with no traffic, my mom in the front seat, my sister and I in the back. I vaguely remember my mom asking my dad to stop somewhere. She had to use the restroom. It was urgent; she had and upset stomach and had to go. One of those "Get me to a bathroom now!" moments we have all had at one time or another. He told her she should have gone before we left, and now, she would wait until we got home. In tears and panic, she begged him to please pull over, anywhere. For more than 30 minutes she cried and moaned in pain trying to hold it in while he yelled at her and insisted this was her fault. She should have gone before we left. He was not stopping, and she would have to wait. And next time she would take care of business before we got on the road. Finally, in her last humiliating attempt, she screamed and cried out, "George, please pull over!" pleading with him one last time. He kept driving. She immediately had an accident in her pants in the front seat of his new car. He continued to drive, with the windows all open, cursing at her for the remainder of the way home. He never pulled over.

My sister and I sat quietly, mortified, in the back seat. When we arrived home a while later, he made her clean the car before he allowed her to clean herself. I learned that day what complete and utter humiliation really was. It's the first time I remember hating my dad. He took us into the house, and my mom spent two hours cleaning herself and Dad's precious car. It breaks my heart writing about it and wishing I was old enough to help my mom or defend her. We never spoke of that incident. I didn't even remember it until many years later. But I'm sure my mother would never forget that Sunday afternoon. God Bless her soul in heaven, I wish I could have told her how badly I felt for her on that Sunday afternoon.

Years later, I realized that my father's anger and verbal abuse towards my sister, Mom, and myself was an instrumental key factor in the development of my lifelong eating disorder. How could it not be? I grew up in fear of him, trying desperately to please him. To be good and stay out of his way. I was looking for his approval, something I have not outgrown.

However, today, I do see him differently, as a hurting human being who was surviving the only way he knew how at the time. I am not blaming; I didn't even comprehend he had been abusive and had anger issues until decades later! Only then could I recognize it and appreciate the effect it had on all of us. I lost my mother over six years ago. I am not very close to my dad as an adult. But I do love him and am able to maintain a father-daughter relationship out of reverence for him. He will not admit or even realize he has a problem to this very day nor, I'm sure, even remember it. I am not asking him to do that. I am keeping a safe distance, protecting myself while still being respectful to an aging parent. The Bible says, "Honor your father and mother… that it may go well with you and that you may live long in the land." (Ephesians 6:2-3 ESV.) I will be obedient and continue to do that.

In the end, his abuse has had a profound effect on the conception of my eating disorder and my lifetime battle with food. I can't say I have forgiven him; there is nothing to forgive. I never blamed him. It was his own coping mechanism in response to his own demons in his life. Something he learned, I am sure from his parents. I was told that my paternal grandmother was an alcoholic and prescription drug abuser, although I do not believe she ever recognized the addiction. It was a long time ago at the end of the Great Depression, when new addictions were being formed to cope with an increasingly changing world. Coming to the realization how extremely detrimental my father's abuse was for me, and the fact that I didn't realize until years later is unimaginable. Or that I married a man with many of the same issues that my own father had is unthinkable. Life is a lesson. Sometimes a very difficult lesson. During the last few years of my mother's life, she used to say something to me every time I left her. She would look into my eyes—she made sure she would find my eyes—and say, "Stay Strong". Like it was important, that life is hard, and I would need those words. She was right.

Chapter 5

School Years

Throughout the rest of my early school years, I continued to develop a very poor conception of my body image. I absolutely considered myself not only overweight but indeed fat, which I had never been accused of, and ugly, which clearly I wasn't. There was a great deal going on in my home. There were secrets, anger, verbal abuse, a cluster of dysfunctions that caused emotional pain. Ultimately, I began to use food to make me feel better in every area of my life. Junior high and high school were miserable years. Although I tried to hide it and pretend I fit in, I never did. I always felt inadequate and insubstantial. I had a few close friends that I would hang out with. However, even back then, I wouldn't allow myself to get too close to anyone, for fear of getting hurt. At the time, I didn't know the reason. That took me years and several relationships to figure out.

I was in the middle group at school. Not in the popular, cool kid's group, which characteristically consisted of the cheerleaders and jocks, and not in the lower group of typical nerds, less physically attractive, and fashion challenged. Right in the middle, convenient. I can get along with everyone and make them happy. I could hold my own on any given day, fitting in, conversing, and laughing with the cool kids while staying close enough to the less popular group in fear of someday landing there. It worked most of the time, although, I secretly always wanted to be popular. I would do anything for their acceptance.

One spring day I let my test paper hang a little too much off my desk for a very popular cheerleader who sat next to me in English class so she could see the answers. Just wanted to help a sista out and again, fit in. She was having a birthday soon and a huge party at her house. She asked me if I would like to go! Would I like to go? Are you kidding? This was my chance at acceptance, being in the IN group. I told her, of course I could make it.

I ran home and told my mom that we must shop for a gift right away. And it had to be a special gift. A gift she would remember! My mom pointed out I didn't even know when or where the party was. I told her I would find out. I trashed my closet looking for the appropriate, special outfit to wear. Not finding anything satisfactory, I insisted to Mom I also needed to buy the perfect outfit. The next few weeks I breezed through school, excited and talking about the big day to all my middle group friends who by the way didn't get an invite! I was the only one!

However, after a few weeks I did not receive a paper invitation. (Pre-computer, – email, – FB, and – Twitter days, real, store-bought, paper party invitations were handed out.) I finally had the nerve during English to squeak out at Popular Birthday Girl that I hadn't received my invitation to her party. She looked at me strangely for a moment. Then realizing the words she had said to me weeks earlier, she rambled something about too many kids, parents set a limit, maybe come for a visit over the summer,. I'm not really sure what else. I didn't hear anything after, "Oh, I'm sorry. I forgot to tell you…" I was completely devasted and completely embarrassed making such a fuss about it to MY friends. It was a huge blow for me, already struggling with an extremely low self-esteem. Of course, I shrugged it off and said, "No big deal." I replied to her that I actually may have had to cancel anyway, having other plans that weekend.

My sister and I were very competitive and fought a lot. More, I believe, then other siblings. I really felt like she despised me. She physically beat me up on a regular basis and would take every opportunity to throw me under the bus and get me in trouble. (Wonder where she got that learned behavior?) I hated her growing up, and many times wished I was an only child. I realize now, she had been fighting her own demons and has also spent her life fighting her own battle with food. Although we have never discussed it, I'm sure she hated me for the simple fact that I was thin. She struggled with being overweight her entire life. Struggling as an overweight child presents an entirely different battle. Children can be mean, and words hurt for a lifetime. She often came home from school crying from the effects of being made fun of.

I remember sneaking smokes with my best friend and my sister telling my parents! She herself was a smoker at the time, and I never said a word. Del would watch me like a hawk for the sole purpose of catching me doing something she could get me in trouble for. I retaliated by doing nothing, ignoring her and trying to keep my distance. There was no way I was going to try to get her back in trouble; that would cause more heartache. I continued my life the same way, ignoring problems and obstacles and going around everything. Trying to keep peace and make everyone like me was a huge effort that facilitated my eating disorder. Eating was the only way I couldn't feel. I refused to feel. It hurt too much. For many years as an adult, I had a magnet on my refrigerator that said, "God doesn't make junk". I would occasionally stop to read those words, thinking how sad that much of my life I had spent feeling that way but also feeling encouraged by those words and knowing deep inside that God did love me and chose me. I just couldn't feel it.

At around the age of 14, I met and began hanging out with an older boy, who I thought was 17, but he turned out to be much older. The fact that my mother had introduced me to him and knew how old he really was only crossed my mind much later as I was forced to evaluate emotional upsets in my life. My self-worth was being tested. My parents were going through a bitter divorce, and my sister and I were living with our father, where we had very little supervision or emotional support. This boy was nice to me. He said nice things to me, made me feel good about myself. Now more than ever, because I wanted to look good for him, I had it in my mind that I was too fat, and for the very first time made myself throw up after a meal. I'm not sure where the idea came from. It was 1977, and eating disorders were relatively new and still not mentioned very often. There wasn't much information at the time. I must have gotten the idea somewhere, probably in school, because at that time, in what should have been a relatively normal pre-adolescent stage of insecurities, when I was most vulnerable, I took control of my life by abusing food. Back then I just thought it was a great diet! A quick way to lose weight! Surely, I would be happy if I were a little thinner! Little did I know that 40 years later, I would still be trying to control my life and my weight the same way. But failing miserably in both areas!

By the grace of God, I didn't get too tangled up with this boy-man, and moved on, but not before it triggered an unrealistic response, an obsession in me that made me want to fit in, to be special, to be thin, but mostly, to be loved. That trigger was the beginning of my long journey with an eating disorder that has raged in me for my entire life.

Consequently, by the age of 14, I began forcing myself to throw up after meals daily. This was not an easy task at first. It took some time and practice to make it happen. But eventually, a short time later, my refluxes began to relax, and I found it easier and easier to "lose a meal." And I started to lose weight! I found a wonderful diet where I could eat anything I wanted and lose weight! Dieting was absurd, eliminating all the foods you loved, weighing and measuring for portion control, eating fruit and melba toast. I was smart. I was in control of my life, and my body! Although I discovered years later it was really about self-hatred and not self-control. Logically, the first few years it was all about losing weight. I didn't attach it to anything else for a very long time. I was a teenage girl; my emotions were all over the place; nothing was logical; it was just a diet. I spent most days thinking about boys and grades and clothes, normal teenage issues. My new secret was just a way for me to keep my weight under control. One less thing to worry about in my stressful life. It never occurred to me that I was using it to stay in control and feel in control of a life full of conflict and pain. Unfortunately, I also learned that excessive eating depresses our spirits even before it destroys our bodies, and I was slowly sinking into an emotional depression.

My mother was clever and eventually caught on to me. I was spending too much time in the bathroom especially directly after a meal. She may have heard me at a certain point. She confronted me and asked why I was throwing up. I panicked, and not knowing how to respond, I told her that I was sick with a virus or something and couldn't stop. Again, this is a time before eating disorders were known or discussed. My mom had no idea I was throwing up to control my weight! And I obviously couldn't tell her that. She would never understand! I didn't fully understand.

She thought I needed medical attention and brought me to the hospital where they admitted me (they were allowed admit people back then) and did several tests: upper GI series, blood work, a sonogram of my stomach. I remember drinking bottles of a horrendous vanilla-flavored liquid chalk for one test which I promptly forced myself to throw up as soon as the test was complete. Ultimately, they sent me home a few days later with no diagnosis. It was probably the flu or a viral infection. I would be okay. Drink lots of liquids and get plenty of sleep. This was the beginning of a very long history of insufficient medical care for a new disease, still misunderstood, misdiagnosed, and mistreated.

I quickly learned, moving forward, that throwing up had to be a secret. I didn't plan to do it much longer anyway. But I wasn't ready to give it up yet. It was working! However, I wasn't losing much weight anymore because I was now eating so much more food than I could get rid of. I did lose a few pounds and was able to maintain my weight and again, eat anything I wanted. That was control! I would just have to get better at hiding it. This began my journey of secret eating, which I still engage in to this day. Not realizing that the longer I went on, the more I became addicted to the huge amounts of carbs and sugar I was eating and the control I thought it brought me. This was a progressive, debilitating disease!

At some point in late adolescence, I must have been tired of the same old routine, and I decided I was going to stop throwing up. Regrettably, after a few days of trying, I realized I couldn't stop. It's the first time I acknowledged that I may have a problem, but I still didn't know how to identify it. It had no name at the time, and I wasn't sure what to do. Life went on as I continued to try and maintain my weight by binging and purging. As time went on, the battle to lose or even not gain weight was clearly going to be a challenge. I was consuming so much food and not purging all of it, ultimately causing me to gain weight. In desperation I would eat even more, which was the beginning of cycle that brought havoc on my body emotionally and physically. I became consumed with it, binging and purging several times a day, every day. My life quickly spiraled out of control and into chaos. The more out of control I felt, the more I ate. It was a vicious cycle that led to a desperation and emptiness in my life, one I could only fill with food. I remember thinking at the time that someday I am going to die, locked in the bathroom alone, clutched to the toilet.

Decades later, I still have this fear. It was also at this time that I began to pray to God for healing, to the God I knew growing up Catholic. A small cry for help to an impersonal God that I barely knew but also feared.

In the book of 2nd Corinthians Paul cried out to God for healing for what he called, "a thorn in my side." Although not specifically identified, he called out three different times and begged God to take it away. Each time God responded, "My grace is sufficient for you, for my power is made perfect in weakness." (2 Corinthians 12:9, ESV) God used Paul in his weakness and in his brokenness. He was never healed in his earthly lifetime.

Chapter 6

Russian Roulette

Through the years, I always despised what I was doing: spending a huge amount of time, effort and money trying to repress my feelings and hide my eating disorder. My sole purpose in life was to lose weight. I realized much later, I am selfish, very selfish. I want what I want, period. I want to eat anything and stay thin at anyone's expense, even my own. Logically, very few thin people stay thin eating anything they want! It has nothing to do with appetite or hunger. I eat whether I am hungry or not! I can count on one hand the times in my entire life that I have felt real hunger. It's all about the food, about the chewing, about the numbing of feelings, the denial of problems. Absurdly, always about the food!

I eat when I am tired, when I have a headache, or if I didn't sleep well, or I have a disagreement with my husband. Food will fix it. Bad day at work, difficult challenge, eat. It's madness! I consciously guard myself against the first dangerous thought. The first, initial thought of eating when I'm not hungry or between a meal when I know, as a food addict, that I can't handle eating between meals. Yet it happens so quickly, I am helpless! As rapidly as I try to fight it off, there is food in my hand, the beginning of a merciless binge. Some days I find myself driving from one fast food restaurant to the next, buying and eating my favorite foods, then purging it all when I arrive home. The result of this lethal combination of selfishness, helplessness, and addiction is a day full of remorse and guilt, another broken promise to God and to myself.

Compulsive overeating is an obsessive addiction of a highly complex nature. The simple fact is that we cannot do without food, and each time the food addict eats, he or she is in danger of surrendering to the compulsion.

I find it a challenge to do anything, to function, to be productive. I must fight every day to get anything done. So much of my energy is spent on my mental obsession with food and the physical effects of overeating, binging, and purging. Writing this book is an enormous project for me to complete. I am praying daily for God to give me the strength and the concentration to put my thoughts on paper in a coherent way. In addition, my chronic neck pain from a neck injury in my 20s and subsequent neck fusion and daily medication keeps me sleepy with very little desire to do anything productive. On many days the pain is so severe that I cannot get out of bed. I have worked on this book in bed on my iPad or on my iPhone when I couldn't sit up to use my desk top computer. It's only with God's grace have I been empowered to complete this book. He keeps pushing me. He continues to speak to me though the Holy Spirit. It is not me who is capable but God's miracle-working power in me. My only motivation comes from the knowledge that if I can't help myself, maybe I can help others. That fact alone keeps me moving forward, knowing that God loves faithful service.

I also understand that one day I may not come out of the bathroom alive. I am playing a huge game of Russian Roulette each time I binge and purge. It's like driving drunk; eventually you will be killed or kill someone else. Knowing this, I continue with this behavior! This disease is insidious!

My addiction has also caused severe memory loss. My memories are spotty at best, almost selective. Some of the memories I have only recently returned in my late adulthood, especially the ones from my childhood. They had been repressed for so many years. I had eaten them into suppression, only to have them reemerge traumatically years later.

Writing this book has taken a huge amount of courage. Baring my secrets to family, friends, and the world is not easy by any reach. Again, God has continued to motivate me, speaking to me and pushing me to complete it for the fundamental reason of helping others. Helping others equals peace, and peace equals eventual healing.

I have bad dreams almost nightly about my childhood, about my eating. My husband is amazed at my dreams, how detailed they are, and how much I can remember after waking in the morning. We often discuss how each dream could have been inspired by recent daily activities. They almost always have my father in them shouting at me with my mom always trying to save me, to help me. One disturbing recent dream had me walking around in public with a toilet lid around my neck! How profound and scary that was to me! I am probably thinking about how this book will bring my secret out to the world. The thought of that disturbs me very much. I am actually scared to death. It's been my lifelong secret, my companion, my friend, and safety net. If I tell, I may be forced to get help. I honestly feel like it's got me beat. I'm too old, too many years in my disease to change. I am selfishly hoping to die this way, with my food.

It's a fact that compulsive overeaters, food addicts, cannot eat the same way as normal eaters. And that's okay! An alcoholic can't drink; drug users can't drug. I get it, I accept it. I accept that I am, and will always be, a compulsive overeater, no matter what my weight is, no matter how ideal my situation is, no matter how perfect my life may be. I can accept the reality that I may have to live with this disease for the rest of my life. Meanwhile, God is using my brokenness to help others.

Compulsive overeating is a permanent, progressive illness. I will never be a normal eater. I must accept this fact and learn how to live with it just as others with other diseases learn to live with their own. I know I can make the right choices. I also have the knowledge and acceptance of my aging body. A body that has served me well over the years and has been kinder to me than I deserved. It's a good body, one that God has blessed me with. A body I have badly abused for decades and continue to abuse because of a compulsion I have not been released from. I pray that one day I could, at the very least, learn to like it just a little.

When we were overeating compulsively, we often tried to hold down our resentment with food. Instead of honestly facing anger and hostility, we tried to make it go away by eating. (Food for Thought, Feb 20.)

Chapter 7

Happily, Ever After

In 1978, at the age of 15, after my father's drug withdrawal, my parent's divorced. My father sold the house, and we moved to a new city further out on the Island. It was my junior year of high school! This event of my life became completely monumental. Having been in the same school my entire life, I was forced to leave all the friends I grew up with from Kindergarten. Friends I have had for over ten years, the only friends I had ever known!

In my new school, I realized very quickly I was not fitting in and skipped classes, barely getting through my last year and graduating. I have not one friend I can remember from this time in that new school, not one. It was during this year or so that my disease progressed enormously, and I became immersed in the food, my weight, and my exceptionally poor self-image. I used incomprehensible demoralization to degrade myself and had thoughts of not wanting to live. Fortunately, I used my eating disorder as an outlet in which I could deal with my emotions. I have been using it as a defense mechanism my entire life, and it's probably saved my life more than once. Good always comes from bad if we allow God to be God and reveal his plan for us. He was taking care of me, although I didn't realize it at the time. As children of a sovereign God, we are never victims of our circumstances. God will always provide a solution in his time.

I did have a new boyfriend and he had a car, a green Chevy Vega. In retrospect, I should have run the other way, but we had fun together. He made me feel good. He said pleasant things to me, and he treated me nicely. I felt like I belonged and that I fit in. I felt loved for the first time in my life. It never occurred to me that I didn't even know what love was! He filled the void in me left by my parent's divorce.

I had successfully been numbing my feelings for a few years by now and wouldn't allow myself to feel anything. What I thought was love was only acceptance and approval and attention. I did have a few close friends at the time; however, I never allowed anyone to get too close to me. I built a nice, tidy wall around myself, keeping secret my binge eating and throwing up and my feelings of inadequacies.

I cried in school and in between classes, in the four entire minutes we had to get to our next class. One of my teachers must have taken notice. I was forced to talk to a guidance counselor and was horrified as I walked in for my appointment and saw my father sitting there! They called my parents! Of course, my mother, not living with us, was not available. My father was the last person I wanted to see there. I can now, as an adult, appreciate his concern and heroic efforts to get there, not being well himself, but at the time I was deeply disturbed and embarrassed. I remember the counselor talking to us both, and I told him I was okay, everything was okay.

I put up a good front for a while. I didn't dare cry in school after that. Or in front of anyone else for that matter. Another secret. Pain should be hidden and not expressed. I used food to repress my feelings and pain more than ever. I ate and sometimes cried while eating but still continued to eat. I refused to let anyone see my vulnerability, to see my pain.

At the age of 17, my boyfriend asked me to marry him, and I said yes. Obviously, my decision-making skills were terrible. I later resented my parents for allowing it. My mom even helped me plan my wedding! I was 17 and was shopping with my mom for a wedding dress, a banquet hall, food caterers…

it was more surreal than exciting. I almost felt she was pushing me to. I probably would have fought her if she told me not to get married, and she knew that once I turned 18, I would do it anyway. But she never once tried to talk me out of it.

I know she had her own hands full at the time, remarried to my dad, and I learned many years later, she had come to regret that decision. She was busy trying to rebuild her shattered life. I realize now I was not getting married as much as I was running away from life. I resented my newly married-again parents who "worked it out" after a few years of divorce and remarried each other, but not until after it had its overwhelming, awful effects on me and my older sister. I am in no way judging. I, myself, have been divorced after 25 years in an unhappy marriage, and I will never condone its horrible effects on the family, especially the children. It is so socially accepted now that I'm not sure how detrimental it is anymore. I'm just saying from personal experience, my parent's divorce was devastating for me.

I wanted to be happy and out of my parents' house. My boyfriend of almost three years, entirely dysfunctional in his own life, promised me a life of happiness. He loved me. He was going to take care of me. Trouble is, he couldn't take care of himself. But I didn't figure that out until years later. We were married on Aug 29, 1981. I turned eighteen on Aug 18th, 1981, a few weeks before, barely being legal. Bad decisions come from fear of doing wrong, with dire consequences. I am so used to being in charge and often forget that God is in charge!

We got pregnant almost immediately, and still eighteen years old, ten months after the wedding (My grandmother was counting.), we had our son. A year or so later and unprepared financially or emotionally, we thought it would be a good idea to have another child. I got pregnant again. This is how I spent my entire life, making bad decisions and choices that had dire consequences and not understanding how my life could be so difficult!

My daughter was born when I was 20, almost two years to the day after her older brother. I had both of my children before my 21st birthday. I was actively in my disease, still not calling it a disease, but perceiving, knowing something was not right. Knowing now that I couldn't just stop or wouldn't just stop. I worried about food a lot and had gained a ton of weight through my pregnancies. I was desperate to get thin again. Throwing up was still working to lose weight. But also included now was my binge eating and then throwing up, which is clearly more than weight control. It was life control. It was my coping mechanism, the way I got through my younger years in my 20s and 30s. I was unhappy, depressed, in an emotionally abusive marriage, raising two children whom I loved dearly. I wasn't old enough or emotionally prepared to be a mother yet, and I was barely getting by. It was by grim determination and resolve to do something about everything. It's how I survived those years trying to appear normal.

Amazingly, I put myself through college during this time. I was determined to be a good mother, always trying to compensate for the inadequacy I felt inside. I cared for my children, always working hard. I was an absolute overachiever, and sadly, I realized at this point, my husband was never going to be able to support us. He was dealing with his own dysfunction from a childhood where he leaned to be selfish and feel self-entitled in which he thought the world owed him a living. He shouldn't have to work so hard for it. In his defense, he always did have a job, but not to the extent where he was paying the bills and taking care of his family. I was the one always pressured to work the extra hours, sometimes a second job, because he wasn't working the "f***king weekend" (even if our rent was late and bills not paid).

During these years, my disease was raging, and I was actively binging and throwing up daily, up to ten times a day or more! I was working full time as a waitress, attending full time college classes, taking care of my children, and trying to endure staying in a marriage that was clearly unhealthy in almost every way. The stress was unbelievable, and I dealt with it by more binging and purging. That was my control over a life that was out of control. I now know that disappointments and pain are a part of God's plans. Through suffering, we come to rely on His, not our own strength. It took me many years to realize this truth.

Did my children suffer because of it? Absolutely. But I did the best I could with what I had. Still, I did not clearly understand that I had a disease or the consequences it would have on my future. My routine consisted of getting up in the morning, (hubby worked the day shift, I worked the swing) making the kids breakfast, getting us dressed, dropping kids at kiddy daycare at the local college, going to my classes all morning, lunch with kids at the daycare, classes in the afternoon, going home, getting ready for work, waiting for my husband to come home from his job so I could run out the door and get to my job on time, then work until midnight! Whew!

It was a grueling schedule that I kept up for some time, eventually switching my work shift to days and part-time college classes at night when my kids were old enough for regular full-time school. Looking back, it's hard to believe I kept that momentum going for so many years, binging and purging several times a day to push any feelings down. I wouldn't allow myself to feel anything. It was too painful. And I managed to stay thin most of the time. Years later I realize that feelings have no power. They cannot dictate my actions. I learned to stop making decisions based on feelings. Unfortunately, I learned this too late.

On my days off, I would pack up the kids and take them to the park or to the beach where we would spend the entire day. I resisted staying at home with the kids. They were happy, healthy, and active children and needed continuous attention. I felt it much easier to keep them busy. I would pack them up and bring them to Lake Ronkonkoma almost daily when the weather was nice. (If that lake sounds familiar, there is a movie being made about it.) There was a small beach area where I could place my chair practically in the water and watch them play. They would drive me nuts at home where I would feel so inadequate trying to care for them and keep them entertained. So I was always somewhere with them doing something. This constant need for activity has stayed with me my entire life. I overanalyze everything, always running, staying busy, possibly running away from myself? Inactivity left me too much time to battle with my feelings. Staying busy was my answer. Staying busy and eating.

I tried to live a normal life or tried to appear to live a normal life, taking care of the kids, trying to stay afloat and on top of the never-ending bills. Life was often chaotic. There were several times we had our utilities turned off, phone (we only had land lines back then) most often, electric, and water on occasion. Someone would eventually come and bail us out, loan us a few bucks to get by. But in my sick mind I thought we were doing okay. I thought this was normal. After all, the kids seemed okay, they were doing well in school, appeared well adjusted and happy.

On the other hand, my marriage was an absolute disaster. I deeply resented my husband's lack of enthusiasm in taking care of his family and his increasing bouts of anger geared towards us due to his own unresolved issues and feelings of self-entitlement. His screaming and yelling were at first just annoying, changing quickly to down-right scary for all of us. I was constantly trying to soothe the kids, keep them quiet, hoping they were "good" so as not to entice his flares of anger. It was a tough job I don't wish on anyone. They were children after all. We were all constantly walking on eggshells. In retrospect, and years later, I realized he was very much like my own father in many ways.

It was about control. It was always about control. I have spent my entire life trying to be thin, thinking that would solve all my problems. Ironically, I wasn't even overweight when my throwing up began. I relied on food to calm me down, console me, and to help me through a bad day. However, it was inadequate, and I had to eat more and more until I became physically and emotionally addicted.

"Because of the LORD's great love we are not consumed, for his compassions never fail. They are new every morning; great is your faithfulness." (Lamentations 3:22-23 NIV)

One of the many emotional problems I was dealing with was fear and anxiety. I had very bad stretches of anxiety and full-blown panic attacks during these early years. So many that I had to seek professional help and take medication to stay calm. Hopelessness is part of this disease. I recognize hopelessness for what it is: my mind protecting me from disappointment. This went on for several years. I suffered terribly from these random attacks and eventually had to be medicated to get through my day. I also sought professional help to try to relieve the symptoms. It was a very dark time in my life. In addition to the daily binging and purging from my eating disorder, I was dealing with another cruel, little-known disease: anxiety disorder. By overeating compulsively, I had deprived myself of good health, self-respect, and peace of mind. By the grace of God, after suffering with them for several years, I read a series of books (that would be extremely out-of-date now) that gave me a new perspective on panic attacks and literally cured me from having them. Except for a few rare occasions, they have totally disappeared. I have, however, continued to suffer from general anxiety on and off over the years, and I always run to my drug of choice, food, for relief. Compulsive overeating always brings back anxieties in full force. I realize without abstinence I will again be overwhelmed and incapacitated by irrational fear and anxiety.

Kim, age two (1965). My first home in the apartment over the candy store.

Kim, age nine, and Del, vacation to New Hampshire 1969. Notice the 1968 Red Chevy Impala in background.

Del and Kim, age ten (1973). Del was thin in this picture. Her weight was always up and down during her childhood.

Kim, age 13, and favorite Uncle Guy at my confirmation.

Kim, age 11, and Woo (1974). Notice book burning fireplace in background.

Mom, Kim (age seven) and Dad. Vacation in Lancaster, PA (1970).

Kim, age nine, Holy Communion (1972).

Del and Kim, age 13 (1976)

Kim,age 12, Christmas (1975).

Kim, age nine, Del, and Mom. Orient Point day trip (1972).

Kim, age 13, and friends in junior high (Hey Peg!) 7th Grade classroom, me on the left, (Clearly, I was not fat!)

Del and Kim, age ten, Easter Sunday at my Grandparents' house across the street (1973).

Del, Mom, and Kim – approx. 1973 (I was about ten.)

My mom and dad, a few months before my mom's death.

Kim, age ten, 5th grade graduation (1973). I went on to win the art award that day!

Kim, 15 years old (1978). I was starting for the first time in my life to gain weight due to the large amounts of food I was consuming. The beginning of Forty Years of Food.

Bill and Kim, Disney Land (2009), first summer we were married. In active disease for over 30 years. My new husband has no idea.

Kim at work (2010), appearing to be normal, dying inside after 30 years of food addiction.

Mom and Kim (2012). My mom passed away at age 69 a few months after this photo was taken.

Kim and Twin Grandsons, Logan and Landon (2015).

My granddaughter, Alexis, age seven—the same age I was when my second-grade teacher made the comment about my weight that would set my eating disorder off (2017).

My grandsons: Bryson, Jack, and Mason (2015).

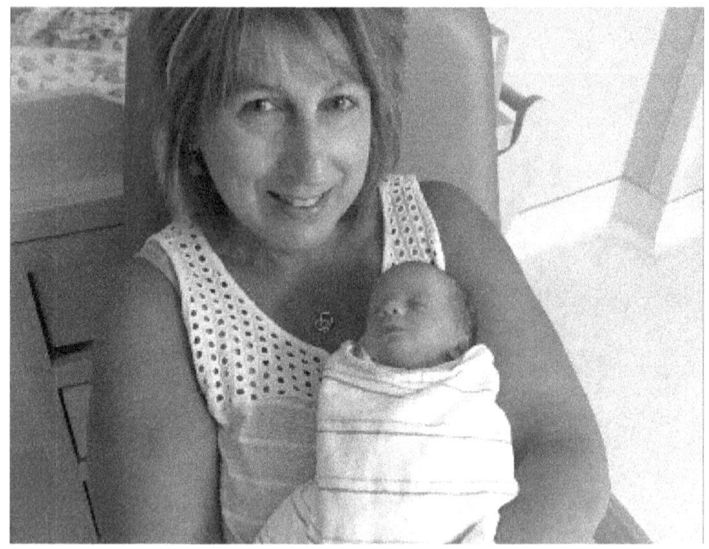

Kim with grandson Logan. I am 52 years old, almost 40 years into my eating disorder and broken on the inside.

My son Matthew with his nephew, my grandson, Landon (2015).

My friend Patty in 2018, whom I met in my early OA days 25 years earlier.

My daughter Mindy with her son, my grandson, Logan (2016).

My granddaughters, Karsyn and Madison (2015).

Chapter 8

Embarrassing Moments

I had several embarrassing moments over the years because of my eating disorder. I used to babysit for two young boys who lived directly across the street from me. I was a little young, but my mom was always home and just a few feet away across the street if I needed her. It was the mid-Seventies, I earned $1.00 per hour for my efforts which in all honesty, I was happy to earn. It was an easy gig. I would go over at bedtime, the boys already in their jammies, play with them for a few minutes then off to bed. Then I would just sit and watch TV.

One night after they had gone to bed, I went to the kitchen looking for a snack. In general, this was not a good snack house, and I knew this. They were of a different nationality and had weird food in their kitchen cabinets. After considerable searching, I did find a frozen chocolate cake in the freezer that was about half eaten. I cut off a small piece just to nibble on. I continued to cut little pieces off to nibble on before realizing I had eaten way too much! It was almost gone! In a panic, I completely cut up the remaining piece of the cake and tried to spread it out in the foil wrapper to make it look bigger. I put it back, and although I worried a little, I really didn't think about it too much after that. Until a few days after, when coming home from school, my mom asked me about the cake. The neighbor eventually discovered her nub of cake in the freezer. I told my mom she was crazy, that I had only a little piece and didn't even like it! The neighbor was exaggerating! That was the very last time I was asked to babysit for them. Appetite grows as it is fed. The more we eat, the more we want to eat.

Several years later, I was working as a waitress on a slow Monday night. It was always just me and one other girl working besides the male cook. That was it. I got into the habit of eating (stealing, although we were technically allowed to eat a normal size meal on our shift) food the entire night, whatever I could get my hands on and not be seen. I remember hiding and eating frozen food inside the walk-in cooler ice box, freezing as I tried to finish it before walking back out! Then I would go into the ladies' employee restroom and purge. I would do this all night. One night I got lazy, instead of going into the lady's stall to vomit in the toilet, I used the garbage can just inside the door of the restroom to do my business, relieving myself of the massive amounts of food I just ate.

I did this for several weeks, thinking it was easier than going into the stall and flushing the bowl three times, but more important, less time consuming (after-all, I was busy at work). I could pop in and out, and no would ever know I was in there for the tenth time of the night.

My clever plan ultimately backfired when I came in for my next shift and discovered, to my dismay, a huge note taped on the mirror right next to the garbage can that said, "Whoever is throwing up in the garbage can, please use the toilet. This is disgusting!" I was mortified and immediately panicked! What would I do! There were always just two woman working Monday night who could have possibly been in the ladies' employee restroom the night before. And I was one of them!

I derived a story to cover myself if anyone confronted me about the incident. The other lady I worked with, a sweet high school girl named Mary Beth, was defenseless against me. I was an overachiever, type A personality, whose fundamental goal was being liked and accepted and could talk my way through most anything back in the day. I was older, married, even had children! Who would they believe? Everyone loved me, and that was essential.

I completely threw her under the bus when my manager approached me and asked if I knew what was going on. I told him that Mary Beth had been sick in the bathroom all night, and I was stuck doing all her work. I acted surprised and then compassionate and told him that now I feel bad that I wasn't more supportive to her last night. Anything to keep my secret! It breaks my heart as I write these words today, remembering what a different person I was back then and how ruthless and secretive this disease can be. To what great lengths I would go to keep it a secret.

Thank God, I accepted Jesus as my personal Savior! He has truly changed that part of me, the angry, self-entitled person who didn't care for others, who always put my needs above those I loved and cared for. It took a few years, but my heart is changed, although God has allowed my eating disorder to continue for all these years. I try to stay faithful and remember that God's time is not my time. Now realizing that the tough lessons I have learned over the years and the compassion I have come to feel for others' anguish from addiction has been a direct result of living with my disease. Although I am still suffering, I am thankful for my disease and the person I have become. By accepting my disease and learning to live with it, I become sane and free in some ways I have never experienced before. Even in disease there can be life, there can be service, there can be peace.

Another time I had been to a buffet with a few friends. (Residing in Las Vegas for the past 25 years, I have had my share of buffets!) They were a bulimic's dream! On one hand, I loved them because of the huge variety of food I could eat. Then, I always felt sad waiting in line to pay, knowing that I would never be able to eat a normal portion, enjoy the company or conversation, but instead would spend most of the mealtime in the casino bathroom. My entire dinner would be focused on the food. How much I could eat and hide, and how many times I could safely get away with going to the restroom. There was a time issue, only a short span of time after eating that I could successfully purge without hurting myself too badly. I have done that often enough over the years in a panic to rid myself of unwanted food and was forced to wait before getting to a bathroom. It's not easy to vomit food that is partially digested and, yes, it physically hurt. I can only imagine the damage it has done to my stomach and throat over the years.

I went through my normal routine of packing as much as I could on my plate and trying to make it not look like too much food. This was a skill I had acquired and could eat almost half of what was on my plate by walking around the buffet for a few minutes before I even returned to the table! One visit, while going through my routine, my girlfriend mentioned that she never did see anyone eat so much food and not be huge! How did I do it? It was a sincere question, and she didn't mean to harm me, but I over-reacted in defense and started rambling on and on about how I hadn't eaten all day, and I don't always allow myself to indulge like this. I probably brought more attention to myself after that response than I needed to. I shut up and made a point of not going to buffets anymore. I couldn't control the amount of food I consumed and other people were beginning to take notice. This was my secret.

At a friend's Super Bowl Party several years ago, I noticed for the first time another food addict. A woman I had met for the first time was there with her husband. I am very aware, especially at a party, of the available food! I begin scanning the room for food I can eat and food I must stay away from immediately. My food addiction also keeps me very aware of how other, normal people eat, and I often try to mimic their eating in hopes of appearing normal myself. I noticed this woman eating a huge meal almost right away, my eyes following her as she made her way to the bathroom. I wondered, but didn't know for sure, if she had an eating disorder. There was an awful a lot of food on her plate for such a little person. My instincts were right as I watched her consume several more plates of food followed by bathroom trips throughout the night! I had also been making my own trips to the bathroom after not being able to withstand the large amount of my favorite binge foods spread all over the room. It's the first and last time I have ever witnessed someone else in active disease, which I was now sure of, binging and purging. It's amazing to me that no one else took notice, absorbed in the party at hand, the good conversation, not in the food served. For a food addict it's difficult to concentrate on anything but the food, which consumes and destroys any possibility of enjoying the party. I often wonder if anyone else did take notice of the two of us, constantly standing by the food table, filling our plates, eating, laughing, pretending to converse, and walking back and forth to bathroom.

There were other moments like the ones above in which I put myself in an embarrassing position while trying to keep my eating disorder a secret. I'm sure there have been many instances where others probably knew something was wrong—too many trips to the bathroom, consuming large amounts of food—that I was not even aware as I tried desperately to keep it hidden.

Chapter 9

Help is on the Way!

It was apparent that I had an eating disorder, which was beginning to be discussed in the news and media. This was early—mid-eighties, pre-internet days—and I got my hands on a book about a young woman suffering from bulimia and her road to recovery. For the first time, I had a name for my disease and, most importantly, realized I was not alone. There were other women suffering from the same thing! That fact in itself was a huge relief.

Through that book and its references, I eventually found my way into the room of an Overeaters Anonymous (OA) meeting which I read about. I saw a listing in the weekly Penny Saver and circled it. I glanced at it a few times during the next few months. Finally, after another merciless day of throwing up, I pulled together the courage to attend a meeting. This is a 12-step program for overeaters, food addicts, and those of us with eating disorders. I knew about Alcoholics Anonymous, at least I had heard about it. I came to find out that OA worked the same as AA except with food instead of alcohol.

When I started going to OA, I jumped in working the program with all my heart, getting my abstinence right away, speaking, writing, working the steps, and going to as many meetings as I could attend. I found a sponsor, called her each day with my food plan, and sometimes during the day when I felt tempted to go off course. I found out soon enough that you must grow or deteriorate. We cannot stand still. And like everything else in my life, I began my recovery full force but gradually fell off the wagon, not working the steps and not being honest with my food. Small adjustments to my food plan led to a huge relapse that I never recovered from.

Over the years I have often wished I were an alcoholic rather than a food addict, which, in my opinion is more difficult to abstain from. After all, we must eat every day! We can't just put down the food and go to meetings. We must eat! We must deal with it at a minimum of three times a day. I compare it to giving an alcoholic three shots of vodka every day, at meal times, and tell them this is all they can have. That may not be a fair analogy, but it's the only way I can explain how difficult it is to abstain from overeating and food addiction. I know because I have been trying to do just that for the last 40 years. I am in no way minimizing the daily battle with which an alcoholic struggles. I personally know a few alcoholics, and the fight they have is merciless. Their drug of choice is alcohol. Mine is food.

I spent nearly two years in those rooms, going to meetings, getting a sponsor, writing down all my food, making phone calls, speaking at meetings, sharing and helping others. For the first time, I had hope. I was finally desperate enough to surrender my life to God. I discovered that I had an actual disease. It's the first time I had heard it called a disease. Something I had little or no control over! So maybe I was sick, and at least I could now justify getting help. I didn't feel so alone anymore. However, the disease continued to rage within me. Knowing that I was suffering from a disease didn't enable me to stop this vicious cycle I had begun several years prior. I needed more help—much more help—but I wasn't willing yet.

In the meeting, I was told that I had to surrender to a Higher Power, whom I chose to call God. Okay, this wasn't too strange for me. I did already believe in God and Jesus and was raised as a Catholic, receiving all my sacraments. I was familiar and comfortable with this. Soon after joining these rooms I acquired a sponsor and started working the program. At some point, with the help of a co-worker who was a Christian and used to witness to me on occasion, my higher power, God, after some time, led me to Jesus, and he became my personal savior. It was a significant moment of my life. I was born again, and my life has never been the same. This was not anything like the Catholic Jesus I thought I knew. This was a personal relationship with Jesus. I was saved and had a new life, a new hope for the future. I had a very long road ahead but this time with Jesus as the driver, not me. I remember these few years as the happiest in my life. I learned that abstinence equals freedom from compulsive overeating and a gift of a new life. The times I stopped using food as a drug allowed me to experience my emotions which I keep buried. I can also feel anxiety, fear, and anger. And joy, enthusiasm, and love. I felt alive instead of doped up.

It should have been easy after that, with the continued love and support of others like myself. I managed several months of what I found was called abstinence. I didn't throw up for over eight months, which was a miracle after almost 16 straight years! I was thrilled! It was many years later before I could realize the real gift was my surrender to Christ as my personal savior. That was life-changing, the beginning of a peace I would carry with me my entire life—not a cure from disease, not immune from difficulties or hardship, but peace within myself. I was desperately clinging to my belief that all things are possible with God!

Unfortunately, this disease is relentless, and happy didn't last too long. As my stress levels increased, I gradually slipped back into my old eating habits. I was learning that Christians suffer hardship and are not immune from difficulties. As my personal life continued to spiral out of control, including a marriage that was riddled with problems, I gradually backed away from the 12-step program. Honestly, I realized that I never fully worked the steps, giving up on myself long before I had a chance. I stopped calling my sponsor each day, stopped writing down my food, completely stopped working the steps. I only got partially through them and sabotaged myself quite often. I resorted back to the self-hatred that I felt way back in the second grade when I stepped off that scale.

I learned that most people are good and caring and will have patience for only so long. In the end, we are on this journey alone. We just want our recovery. No one is going to babysit us. Everyone has their own lives, their own problems. I took their lack of response of saving me personally and quit going all together. But not before my disease was back in full swing. Almost two years into the program I left those rooms for good and haven't been back. That was over 25 years ago. My ultimate fail was after all the years of binging and purging to stay thin, for all my efforts, I am overweight! How ironic, I failed at my own disease which was supposed to keep me thin, which was supposed to make me happy.

I always felt I had control over my life when I was throwing up. It was my defiant "NOTHING can hurt me" defense mechanism. If I looked at my problems, I may have to work on them and admit to them. I wasn't willing to do that. I'm not sure I ever will. I went back to my lifestyle, for the most part, without my program friends whom I grew to love. I would never allow anyone to get too close. I always keep my distance. I don't want anyone to know my secrets, to figure me out.

I received, however, a very important gift from those rooms, a gift far more important than my abstinence from food addiction, a gift I am eternally grateful for. That's my relationship with Jesus Christ, which has grown and strengthened over the years as I have matured in my faith. Perhaps, that was God's plan all along. When I really let go and start trusting, God has an opportunity to correct what seems hopeless to me. He loves me right where I am today. One of the mottos from OA to was keep what you want and leave the rest. I chose to do that with my salvation. It takes courage to change, to become a new person. To move forward doing God's work, in spite of disease and pain, requires courage. The painful years have been a life-work, preparation for service and helping others. It's a blessing from God.

Chapter 10

Through the Years

During this time as I worked at completing my degree in Business Management, I landed an incredible job with a major retailer as a department training manager. It paid quite well (and fed my extremely low self-esteem). I thrived on the pressure, the hours I worked, and having to travel for business. I was not only smart, but I was so cool now, too! I had several employees working for me, and I felt very important. I was still very young, about 30, and very immature. I loved my new career, which lasted over the course of several years. For the first time in my life, I had the opportunity to travel and to meet people.

Of course, I know now that wasn't what is important in life. I literally cry today as I think of the lost time with my children—by my own choice—and how much they needed me. I can never forgive myself for that time. I had extreme access to food with a daily food allowance at my new job and alone time, the combination was deadly for a bulimic. As an over-achiever, type-A personality, I excelled and was promoted quickly several times. However, three years into my dream job, my bulimia was so bad I was forced to seek medical help. Up until this point, besides the old friends from my OA days, no one knew, not even those close to me, my husband, my sister, my parents, children, no one! It was still my secret.

I was eventually hospitalized for my eating disorder. As I struggled to keep up at work my body was breaking down, and I was admitted into Princeton University Hospital's eating disorder/substance abuse program. No one in my family knew the reason. I was traveling for business and told them it was for the flu-like symptoms I had been having for months which was finally diagnosed conveniently at the same time as Graves' disease.

The stress of traveling, being away from family, marital problems, financial problems, poor decisions had led to my bulimia spiraling out of control. I was binging and purging all day, every day, and my body was suffering the physical effects as well as the emotional effects. Although in retrospect, the binging and purging probably saved my life. Emotionally I was a wreck, and the eating disorder became my defense mechanism against my many problems while trying to work and keep up the appearance of a self-confident, knowledgeable employee dedicated to her job. In secret, I was falling apart, sneaking food all day and then finding different bathrooms to purge in. I had the luxury of working independently, coming and going as I pleased, and I used that benefit to fuel my eating disorder

I was admitted to the four-week inpatient program for a variety of addictions. I was in the "Eating Disorder Unit". We all had a scheduled itinerary each day of individual and group counseling, OA meetings, physical activity, everything to help you recover. It was supposed to be a 30-day program, very rigid. We followed a strict schedule of eating meals together, learning proper nutrition, proper portions. I did learn a great deal about food at this time, such as, which foods were good to eat and how bad foods affected your health. I was extremely knowledgeable about nutrition and food! But that knowledge couldn't solve my problem! I was addicted to food. Carbs and sugars, I could binge on whole wheat toast! It didn't matter. The binging and purging, and this is important, were only a symptom of what was really going on inside. Until I dealt with the reason I was numbing myself, I couldn't get well. I wouldn't get well. I laughed at the program, and the counselors. They had no clue as to what went on inside a food addict's head, or any addict for that matter. I spent my entire time there, doing as little as possible, avoiding any real therapy that could help, and tricking the hospital staff.

The problem was that I looked normal. I often would sneak out of the locked ward, walking behind an attendant who was exiting. I was never questioned. I didn't look like a patient. I walked into the employee cafeteria several times a day and purchased any kind of food I wanted!

We followed a rigid schedule of group and individual therapy. Every afternoon we would sit in a circle of about 15 women. We shared our individual horror stories of food addiction. Women of different sizes and nationalities. We laughed. We cried. Mostly we cried. I remember listening to the young girls' stories of their own struggles with anorexia, how they wouldn't eat anything all day! All week! Yet their disease emotionally was the same as mine, although the symptoms were a world apart!

I remember one of the counselors, a woman younger than me. I didn't want to hear the other stories. I didn't want to be there at all. My counselor was missing an arm. I stared at it, or where it should have been, the entire time, wondering how she lost it and how it had affected her life. I wondered if she was married, had children, totally concentrating on the pain in *her* life for only having one arm. I spent a lot of time feeling sorry for her, for her life instead of feeling that sorrow for myself, the losses I have had because of my disease. I chose to stay behind a wall of self-righteousness, although I knew I was in trouble. I hid behind the wall.

Admittedly, most of the patients consisted of teen girls and young women. There was a man on our ward in his early 30s. Turned out he was a "cutter" and couldn't control his impulses to hurt himself. In retrospect, they probably didn't have a place specifically to put him; "cutting" was less known about back in the 80s, more than newly discovered eating disorders. We would chat in between our individual itineraries and discovered we had a lot in common. He felt unworthy, and cut himself, hurt himself. I binged ate and threw up to hurt myself. We had more in common than anyone would have thought. We spent the next few weeks chatting with promises of keeping in touch. That was the last I ever heard of or saw of Dan. I have often wondered over the years if he was able to get relief from himself.

We also had measured and group meals each day. Grouped together with our list in hands of what foods and how much we could have, we planned our meals with the menu of the day. With the help of our leader, we went thru the cafeteria line choosing our approved items and making our plates.

During my individual counseling sessions, I recall talking around everything and never going too deep. Everything was fine, I'm definitely learning how to choose and eat healthy foods (which I was), and I was recovering nicely! It was a lot of nonsense that I knew she would want to hear, to write on her yellow tablet, none of it true. I had the knowledge, regarding what I should eat and how much, but I also had the addiction, the obsession of food addiction.

I even convinced my roommate's mother to bring me food! Her daughter, a shy girl in her late teens, had anorexia as well as OCD. I promised her mother if she brought food I would get her to eat it. Then I ate it all! My roommate told her mom that she was eating it. Some of the same tricks alcoholics use but with food. Addiction is addiction! Living without the narcotic of excess food means learning to cope with emotional pain. I didn't know any other way to deal with the pain of my life.

I often left the entire hospital, just walking out the main entrance. I walked a few blocks to Main Street, where I could indulge in fast food or spend time in coffee shops eating donuts and carbs to my delight. Not surprisingly, I failed miserably there. I pretended to be the ideal patient, but snuck around, buying and stealing food and then purged in the doctor's restroom facility. The patient bathrooms in the eating disorder unit were strictly guarded and without doors so they could watch and make sure we weren't doing just that!

The hospital program also failed miserably by underestimating how insidious this disease could be and what lengths people will go to for their drug of choice. In their defense, it was the mid-80s, and food addictions were just starting to be taken seriously and considered a disease. There was so much still to be learned back then.

Halfway through my four-week stay, I was diagnosed with Graves' disease, explaining my long bout with flu-like symptoms that had occurred consequently over the last several months. My hospital stay for bulimia was cut short. The Graves' disease was in advanced stages, and I was transferred by ambulance to Princeton University hospital for a five-day stay and a thyroidectomy. I am convinced the onset of this autoimmune disease was directly related to the previous fifteen years of binging and purging and abuse to my body. In any event, I was treated there for a week and released. I went home (now taking one pill a day for life to supplement not having a thyroid), went back to work and back to my disease.

My job continued to keep me busy, and I buried myself in it. But I became bored and my productivity was affecting my job performance. I eventually left and moved on to other jobs, all that I truly liked and excelled at. I made many friends over the years, though I would be hard-pressed to remember many of their names. But I always remember their faces and their kindness. It's as if they knew I was broken inside without knowing why. The continued binging and purging allowed me to keep the feelings repressed and pushed down so I couldn't feel the pain of life.

I was raising my children, trying to set good examples with my faith, but failing in so many other areas. My marriage was becoming unbearable. My husband, also struggling with his own battles of inferiority, was also trying to survive. Eventually he stopped working an ordinary job, insisting he would never work for someone again. He depended on small odd jobs to keep him going. Both of us were looking out for our own needs.

As a last attempt to find happiness, we moved to Las Vegas from Long Island, where his family lived. We tried to begin a new life, purchased a home, and started a family business that we ran together for several years. Ironically, it was a potato chip business! Of course, always staying in line with my food addiction and the food to fuel it.

What should have been a proud and exciting time became one of the most difficult periods in our marriage. The business lacked working capital, it grew quickly and couldn't sustain itself. We borrowed and mortgaged our home but couldn't hold it together. Struggling to the bitter end, we ultimately lost our home and filed bankruptcy. After 25 turbulent years of marriage, we divorced. I am deeply saddened by my divorce and divorce in general. It is never good for the children, knowing first-hand how disruptive it can be and how extremely painful it is for everyone involved. I will never condone it. God hates it. But it does happen, for good reasons and bad. It's part of our new culture where most anything is accepted. I have watched my own child go through a painful divorce and my grandchildren struggle through it. Life does go on. They are living proof of that and have adjusted quite well to their new two-home situation.

I am living proof that healing can occur and did find peace after my divorce. Removing myself from this chaotic relationship enabled me to breathe again and try to take care of myself. Frightened as I was, I found a sense of relief being alone and making my own decisions. I didn't realize how much control I allowed my ex-husband to have on me and my life. Although saddened, I did not regret ending the marriage.

Regret is not something I wanted to use to torment myself, which I could easily do. I forced myself to move forward, remembering my past but not being too hard on myself depending on and recognizing God's mercy. Change is characteristic of all growth.

I will also make myself learn tolerance, kindness, patience, courtesy, and love. I have a firm determination to do what is necessary to improve my life. I have a responsibility to myself to live at peace with others and with myself!

Chapter 11

Pat Said YES!

The years continued quickly on. My children, now grown, had lives and children of their own when I remarried a wonderful man in June 2009. Despite the best intentions, it is difficult for one who is not a compulsive overeater to understand and help one who is. I was fearful that my new husband wouldn't understand, and my insecurities led me to keep it a secret throughout our marriage.

Often, we do not see the ultimate results of our actions. However, my disease continues to be unrelenting. The habits and addiction have already been formed and practiced for many years. I went into my new marriage with the same old emotional baggage I carried my entire life. Unfortunately, a new husband didn't cure my disease. But as I aged, I became more peaceful and although still very much active in my disease, felt a new happiness never felt before. Through maturity and God's grace, I was learning what true love is.

We purchased a home and began our lives together. Shortly after getting married, my husband Bill, a Christian man, and I were watching a TV show that we had only been watching for a few weeks called *The 700 Club*. I found out later that it's been around for many years and that Pat Robertson is the host. They have a segment where a viewer emails a question and Pat and the co-host will answer live. One day after only watching the show for a few weeks, and not on a regular basis, I felt the urge to ask Pat a question. I went to their website and clicked the link to send a question in. I asked Pat, "Can a person who is an active addict still be considered saved?".

I was questioning my faith, thinking in in the back of my mind that I wasn't saved because I was active in my addiction. After all, I have promised God so many times in the past that I would stop abusing my body, the one He gave me to live my earthly life in. But I never managed to keep my promise. I sinned each day, and although I repented, I never fully turned from my sin. I kept doing it! I needed to break out of my own self-centeredness, being completely absorbed in my own issues and appetite, and start focusing some attention on the concerns of those around me. Tough lesson, the world does not revolve around me.

Unbelievably, that same day, (and again, we were not watching it regularly, or even looking for it at that time) we just happened to finish dinner that night and sat in front the TV when *The 700 Club* came on. They soon came to the email question segment. The very first question Pat read was my question! From that same day! I just emailed it to them hours earlier! I almost fell out of my chair. Of course, not letting my husband know, because it was still a secret, I listened intently as Pat read my question, "from Kim in Las Vegas, 'Can a person still be saved if they are actively in their addiction?'." I am paraphrasing him, but he answered very plainly, "Of course you can, but why would you want to be? God will give you the power and grace and can set you free." I remember saying to myself for days and months afterward, "Pat said YES! "I wrote it in my journal, so I wouldn't ever forget that moment. It was a profound moment to say the least! And I couldn't celebrate with anyone! But now I can! Pat said yes! I silently praised God.

Another time, while at work and listening to a Christian radio program, I decided to call in and ask the pastor radio host a question. I asked him a similar question about being an active addict and if that affected my salvation. I was concerned for my salvation. He gave me a similar answer. I was again relieved but not convinced. How can God always forgive me?

I was now also afflicted with debilitating and severe chronic pain issues due to an old neck injury I had when I was much younger. I was 20-something when after an accident, the resulting pain it caused subsided for several years, and I could function. But at 40-something the pain became unbearable which resulted in a botched neck surgery, a fused spine and the beginning of my lifetime of current chronic pain that eventually led me to disability. I fought this for a few years, but ultimately, I realized I just couldn't function at work.

It was a very depressing time for me, which led to several unsuccessful attempts at curing and now, managing the pain. In retrospect, I am sure my years of abuse towards my body added to my severe pain issues. There were times when I would give my body a reprieve and not binge for a few days at a time. The only time I had ever been successful is when I totally gave up sugar and refined flour, bread, carbs; basically, what I consider the good stuff. It's all the food I am addicted to! In my mind, I know if I ever want to have abstinence again I will have to work at it, give these foods up.

But that's not the entire story. Emotionally, I have to have the willingness and desire to stop, and after all these years, if I want to be truthful, I don't want to have to work at it. It is my comfort. I often ask God to take it from me, miraculously, so I don't have to work at it. And it gets more complicated. I realize now, it's not just the food. I am compulsive about everything. I have an addictive personality. I run from one extreme of excess busyness to keep my mind off myself, to complete and utter fatigue and not being able to do anything. I try not to yield to laziness or defeat. All around me are the evidences of a loving God who will help me if I allow it. God says to trust him, for He cannot or will not fail us.

"Many of us have spent most of our lives dreaming of the day when we would be thin and attractive and able to do the things we want to do. We have put off living to some indefinite time in the future. As long as we were fat, we had a reason to avoid challenges and delay satisfactions. By not attempting to realize our dreams, we averted the risk of failure and the possibilities of success”. (Food for Thought, Aug 16)

Chapter 12

A New Beginning

I have done some things in my past, even as a Christian, that I am very embarrassed by. Some things that I would be hard pressed to admit or talk about now. Unbelievable things that bring me shame even today, years later. Decisions that were disastrous. In life there are neither rewards nor punishments, but there are consequences. Good consequences when you live the life God calls you to live and bad consequences when you make poor decisions against God's will. I am living proof that God brings peace and healing through his grace. Only He has the power to restore us and bring healing to our lives. No situation is hopeless. We are never victims of our own circumstances! God is control of our futures. You can move forward doing God's work even in the midst of pain and disease.

Wisdom is the ability to live life in complete submission to God's direction and principles. I pray for wisdom each day. Even after repenting and changing my ways and knowing that Jesus forgives me, I can't forgive myself. I cry over the stupid decisions I have made. I pray the same prayer to God over and over. "Here I am again Lord, stumbling over the same sin. I'm so tired of losing this battle, and you're probably tired of forgiving me. Thank you for never giving up on me, as I give up on myself daily." Then I remember God's promises to me: "The Lord, The Lord, a God merciful and gracious, slow to anger, … forgiving iniquity and transgression and sin." Exodus 34:6-7 (ESV). I also know the only way to make amends for past mistakes is to live the right way today!

I read examples of God's mercy in the Bible stories of the Old Testament. David, a man after Gods own heart, a righteous man, who loved God with all his heart, the author of the Psalms was a sinner! He lied, committed adultery, even had a man murdered! Yet God forgave him, used him, and had a purpose for David's life. It is through his seed we were promised our savior, Jesus Christ.

Elijah's rescue came only after the brook dried up. (1st Kings 17) He had to endure to the end, and God saved him and took him up to Heaven. He didn't give up but trusted wholly in God.

God spoke to Moses from the burning bush. Then he spent 40 years wandering in the wilderness because of the sins of Israel. But those were not wasted years; God was planning for him. He was being used; God was preparing him for service. When Moses was ready, and his brokenness had reached its goal, God brought him to his fulfilment. Although he would never cross over to God's promised land, he would lead the Israelites to the land God promised to them. Moses's life had meaning. My life has meaning.

Like Moses, our years are not being wasted, and God has a plan for us. We may have many wilderness years too, years where our sin far outweighs our service. In those years God is shaping us and teaching us. We may never see the results in this lifetime, but the effects of those years will be remembered and left with our loved ones and those we witnessed to. Jerimiah 29:11, one of my favorite bible verses says, "For I know the plans I have for you," declares the Lord, "plans to prosper you and not to harm you, plans to give you hope and a future." (NIV) My hope is in the future, here on earth and finally in my eternal home, heaven.

Out of pure frustration of not being able to take off any weight, I joined Weight Watchers last summer. I have never had success with any diet or weight loss program, having tried everything in the past to lose weight. For the first time in my life I am learning to eat healthy, what correct portions look like, and how to eat a balanced healthy diet. It was easier than I anticipated. Food converts to points. Based on your initial evaluation of your current height and weight and exercise patterns, you are given a certain amount of points to eat daily. Once you hit your goal weight, your points will increase to maintain your weight. Exercise will increase your daily points. There are also weekly points that are in addition to your daily points that you can spend on any food you want to eat.

Unbelievably, I have had some success with Weight Watchers, losing twenty pounds over the summer! This is the first time in several years I have been able to take off any weight. The ease of the online app and emotional support has kept me encouraged. This is a great weight loss program! Unfortunately, my eating disorder, still active, continues to triumph over any success that I do have. I am binging and purging almost daily, more so for comfort and familiarity, than a weight loss tool. Although I have managed to keep the twenty pounds off, I'm at a standstill right now and actively in my disease, even as I try to complete my book. I do have many more good days now than I have ever had, with the binges less frequent. That in my mind is progress. Progress equals peace. But peace does not always equal healing. I carry a sadness with me for a life filled with so many losses.

My disease has held me back, preventing many blessings from coming into my life. I know this because I continue to suffer the consequences of bad decisions I have made due to lack of trust and confidence. In an unending desire to please others and make myself look good, I have done things that I am saddened by. I am still trying to diet to manipulate and control my food and weight, always certain that I will be happy when I am thin! I continue to get a temporary high from food (my choice of drugs), but invariably I overeat and end up feeling worse than before! I can't seem to get out of my own way. Each day I reminisce about my life and the "should haves" that I continually think about, which seem to reinforce and acknowledge my failures. Failures keep me in my disease with no willingness to fight for my life. The solutions rest with me. The poor financial decisions, the poor relationship decisions, decisions I made raising my children, job and business opportunities lost. Forever. The list is endless. Ultimately, I am hardest on myself, knowing there is no one to blame, although I have tried to push my iniquities on others for many years. Happiness cannot be achieved by pursuing it. Happiness is the direct result of living the right kind of life.

I once read that, "courage isn't the absence of fear, it's the strength to carry on in spite of fear"! I am realizing that it's not my circumstances that need change as much as myself. Once I change myself, the circumstances will certainly change. I am learning how to be honest. No more pretending to be what I am not. My body is where it is; its size and shape is between me and God and is no one's else's business. I wish I could have seen that as a teenager when my goal to please and fit in was raging.

My morning prayer time is difficult for me. I cry a lot. I reflect on the things I have done and on those I failed to do. I am sorry, yes, but my life cannot be changed now. However, I can make restitution to myself and to those I hurt by living a new life today. By trying to live the right life today for God.

With that being said, I have a progressive disease that will get worse over time. It's an addictive illness that is of a highly complex nature. I lose compassion for myself, for this illness of my mind and spirit. For all the food I consume in a day, I always go to bed hungry, and I tell myself I deserve that. I deserve pain for not doing what is right and not being able to keep my promise to God.

Furthermore, as of today, as I write these words, those close to me, my husband and best friend, my grown children, and my friends have no idea that I live with this disease. I'm undecided at this point if I will even put my name on this book! Maybe I should publish it anonymously. I'm embarrassed and worse yet, I may be forced to get help. I'm too old for this. And I am still not willing!

As I struggle to complete a book that I had no intention of writing, I can hear God's voice asking me to finish it. Asking me to work on it a little every day. He needs me to help others through this book. I am still very active in my disease and feeling sad. I don't want to give up the food. It's been my coping mechanism for almost half a century. It's too hard for me. In my humanness I don't think I can do this. I have recently dug out and began reading my old OA books and literature. It's a life-saving program. I realize I have missed my opportunity in my younger years to be willing to work it. I believe that knowledge is power. I have ultimate knowledge regarding my disease, but no power to overcome it! By the grace of God there is still hope for me to have complete healing in my lifetime.

I don't have a solution or cure for my addiction. I won't agonize. I may not receive healing in my lifetime. Hopefully writing this book, obeying God's voice, to help others will ultimately help me to be able to look in the mirror and say, "Kim, you're okay."

I am also living proof of the healing God brings through his grace. God's unconditional love heals, restores, and makes things new. I have a new beginning every morning. Know that God can take your life, no matter how bruised and broken, and make something beautiful out of it.

I would like to end this book saying I am healthy, that there is hope for healing. The truth is that I am still suffering daily from the effects of this awful disease. My disease is still active, and I battle to get though each day. But there is always hope. God does answer prayer. There is always hope for complete healing. Hope that this book will help others realize they are not alone and seek help for themselves. Hope that we can still live a whole life, peaceful and content and in disease with God's love. Our broken lives have meaning. We can serve God today in any condition.

Epilogue

If you are looking for a happy ending or a cure for food addiction, sadly, I do not have it. Never, in all the years of fighting it, did I think I would admit to being defeated by food. Yet here I am, a 55-year-old grandmother, still struggling and actively suffering from this cunning and baffling disease. Anyone who enters my life will not get past the point at which my secret begins.

Like alcoholism and drug addiction, there isn't a cure for food addiction. But that does not mean hope is gone! There is hope! Hope for progress, for improvement for a life lived fully, as fully as can be lived, with addiction. And there is healing, maybe not complete healing, but some healing. I will not let my destiny destroy me. I won't wait to be cured to be happy.

My childhood friend Peg, who proofread my manuscript and wrote the foreword to this book, commented about the ending, "Such a sad, defeated tone at the end. You have dedicated this book to your daughter and granddaughters! What is the message you want to send to them? Are you telling them you give up? I don't think you are".

Very good question Peg! I don't want to convey a message of lost hope, of giving up. But I am here still very much a food addict, very much still in my disease. Maybe the message is that I have wasted forty years of my life, forty years NOT living my life to the fullest, because of this disease. Realistically, I may never get well! Do I stop living my life because of my addiction? Maybe my message is to live fully each day regardless of your situation and in spite of addiction! My hope and prayers are always for complete, total healing. I pray that God can use my life of food addiction to help others, that my time here on earth isn't for nothing but has meaning and lessons for someone.

I am very frustrated, and I have struggled trying to complete this book. I see now that God has a plan for me, for my book. After several months of extensive binge eating, I am allowed a reprieve. Almost two weeks of abstinence, expect for one small slip and back on track, with Weight Watchers which out of complete desperation, I joined again. After some success last summer, I have lost and managed to maintain a 20-pound weight loss for almost a year. I have recently regained four pounds. Not wanting to give back my hard work, I enrolled in WW again. I have followed the point system faithfully and have re-lost the four pounds and gained a new abstinence which I haven't had since I left WW almost a year ago. WW does work for me, not so much for the plan and discipline it requires, but to keep me from overeating, which almost always results in binge eating and purging.

My husband, having now read my manuscript, obviously is aware of my eating disorder and food addiction. It was very difficult for me to allow him to read my book. But I know that letting go of secrets is a key to recovery. He probably doesn't completely comprehend the complexity of my disease. But he is a loving, supporting husband who will do anything to help me get better. I am slowly talking to him about it, and he is learning how insidious a disease it is. I'm pretty sure he wonders each time I go into the bathroom, especially after meals, what I am doing in there. Which I agree, he probably should. For the first time in my life, I am being held accountable and must answer to someone for the food I eat. I admit, I am not happy about that. It could force me to put effort into getting well. I am not ready to give up my food! I do not want to feel. NOT now, not ever. I am comfortable in my own misery

I do need structure and discipline for my daily eating. One bite off of my food plan and my head is in the toilet. I must remember this! I like being abstinent, losing a little weight, feeling good, and enjoying life. In the same way, I DO always feel a loss! I love my FOOD so much! I miss eating my food. I am saddened that I can't have it, although on Weight Watchers I can eat any food as long as I track it! But I am truly NOT capable of eating a small slice of pie or a few cookies! That would put me in a total binge for days or weeks! Normal eaters can probably do that to a certain degree, although I have a feeling there are not too many normal eaters in Weight Watchers. People join because of their frustration for not being able to lose weight. For their lack of control. I am sure lack of control is something all overeaters have in common, not just those with eating disorders.

I want, desire, to help others! Others who suffer from eating disorders. But I often ask myself how I can help others when I can't help myself? My only answer is through my experiences with my own eating disorder. Active or not, I still have valued experience that can help others. I have also decided to try OA again. I had limited success 25 years ago and am willing to give it another try. I realize that recovery is often found with the help of others who suffer from the same disease.

I am appreciating that I don't need to continue to punish myself for past mistakes, either by overreacting or by denying my legitimate right as an individual to receive forgiveness. I can see God working mightily in and through me to accomplish his purposes.

Since I didn't respect myself, I did not act in a way which evoked respect from others. I allowed other people to use me. I am learning that self-respect is an inner acceptance that is more important than any external approval or disapproval. I am learning to take care of my body physically and emotionally. Each day is a blessing and a lesson.

In the book of Romans Paul writes, "Not only so, but we also glory in our sufferings, because we know that suffering produces perseverance, character; and character, hope." (Romans 5:3-4)

Though pain comes hope. Hope for healing and sometimes hope to shift my focus away from my own discomfort and troubles, and towards helping others. This is my prayer.

Information about Eating Disorders

Bulimia nervosa is a psychological and severely life-threatening eating disorder described by the ingestion of an abnormally large amount of food in short time period, followed by an attempt to avoid gaining weight by purging what was consumed.

Methods of purging include forced vomiting, excessive use of laxatives or diuretics, and extreme or prolonged periods of exercising. Often, in these binge/purge episodes, a woman or man suffering from this disorder will experience a loss of control and engage in frantic efforts to undo these feelings.

Since he or she may have binging and purging episodes in secret, they are often able to conceal their disorder from others for extended periods of time. Those suffering from bulimia nervosa often utilize these behaviors in an attempt to prevent weight gain, to establish a sense of control, and/or as a means of coping with difficult circumstances or situations.

Major Types of Bulimia

There are two common types of bulimia nervosa, which are as follows:

- **Purging type** – This type of bulimia nervosa accounts for the majority of cases of those suffering from this eating disorder. In this form, individuals will regularly engage in self-induced vomiting or abuse of laxatives, diuretics, or enemas after a period of binging.

- **Non-Purging type** – In this form of bulimia nervosa, the individual will use other inappropriate methods of compensation for binge episodes, such as excessive exercising or fasting. In these cases, the typical forms of purging, such as self-induced vomiting, are not regularly utilized.

Causes of Bulimia

The exact cause of bulimia nervosa is currently unknown; though it is thought that multiple factors contribute to the development of this eating disorder, including genetic, environmental, psychological, and cultural influences. Some of the main causes for bulimia include:

- Stressful transitions or life changes
- History of abuse or trauma
- Negative body image
- Poor self-esteem
- Professions or activities that focus on appearance/ performance

Bulimia Treatment

Since negative body image and poor self-esteem are often the underlying factors at the root of bulimia, it is important that therapy is integrated into the recovery process. Treatment for bulimia nervosa usually includes:

Discontinuing the binge-purge cycle: The initial phase of treatment for bulimia nervosa involves breaking this harmful cycle and restoring normal eating behaviors.

Improving negative thoughts: The next phase of bulimia treatment concentrates on recognizing and changing irrational beliefs about weight, body shape, and dieting.

Resolving emotional issues: The final phase of bulimia treatment focuses on healing from emotional issues that may have caused the eating disorder. Treatment may address interpersonal relationships and can include cognitive behavior therapy, dialectic behavior therapy, and other related therapies.

Source: **https://wwweatingdisorderhope.com**

I recommend eatingdisorderhope.com for sound information on eating disorders and how to diagnose and get help for yourself or a loved one.

My choice method has always been binge eating and purging. Although I have several "trigger" foods. I can and have binged on almost any food. I can hide my disease because I have managed to maintain a normal or slightly above normal body weight throughout the years. My obsessive eating and purging is often driven by emotion and stress, and self – hatred.

Binge eating disorder (BED) is a severe, life-threatening, and treatable eating disorder characterized by recurrent episodes of eating large quantities of food (often very quickly and to the point of discomfort); a feeling of a loss of control during the binge; experiencing shame, distress, or guilt afterwards; and regularly using unhealthy compensatory measures (e.g., purging) to counter the binge eating. It is the most common eating disorder in the United States.

BED is one of the newest eating disorders formally recognized in the DSM-5. The change is important because some insurance companies will not cover eating disorder treatment without a DSM diagnosis.BED is a fairly new term used with Eating Disorders. It's linked very closely and contains some of the very same symptoms as bulimia.

Diagnostic Criteria

- Recurrent episodes of binge eating. An episode of binge eating is characterized by both of the following:
  - Eating, in a discrete period-of-time (e.g., within any two-hour period), an amount of food that is definitely larger than what most people would eat in a similar period of time under similar circumstances.
  - A sense of lack of control over eating during the episode (e.g., a feeling that one cannot stop eating or control what or how much one is eating).
- The binge eating episodes are associated with three (or more) of the following:
  - Eating much more rapidly than normal.
  - Eating until feeling uncomfortably full.
  - Eating large amounts of food when not feeling physically hungry.
  - Eating alone because of feeling embarrassed by how much one is eating.
  - Feeling disgusted with oneself, depressed, or very guilty afterward.
- Marked distress regarding binge eating is present.
- The binge eating occurs, on average, at least once a week for three months.
- The binge eating is not associated with the recurrent use of inappropriate compensatory behaviors (e.g., purging) as in bulimia nervosa and does not occur exclusively during the course of bulimia nervosa or anorexia nervosa.

Warning Signs & Symptoms of Binge Eating Disorder

Emotional and behavioral

- Evidence of binge eating, including disappearance of large amounts of food in short periods of time or lots of empty wrappers and containers indicating consumption of large amounts of food.
- Appears uncomfortable eating around others
- Any new practice with food or fad diets, including cutting out entire food groups (no sugar, no carbs, no dairy, vegetarianism/veganism)
- Fear of eating in public or with others
- Steals or hoards food in strange places
- Creates lifestyle schedules or rituals to make time for binge sessions
- Withdraws from usual friends and activities
- Frequently diets
- Shows extreme concern with body weight and shape
- Frequent checking in the mirror for perceived flaws in appearance
- Has secret recurring episodes of binge eating (eating in a discrete period-of-time an amount of food that is much

larger than most individuals would eat under similar circumstances); feels lack of control over ability to stop eating

- Disruption in normal eating behaviors, including eating throughout the day with no planned mealtimes; skipping meals or taking small portions of food at regular meals; engaging in sporadic fasting or repetitive dieting
- Developing food rituals (e.g., eating only a particular food or food group [e.g., condiments], excessive chewing, and not allowing foods to touch).
- Eating alone out of embarrassment at the quantity of food being eaten
- Feelings of disgust, depression, or guilt after overeating
- Fluctuations in weight
- Feelings of low self-esteem

Physical

- Noticeable fluctuations in weight, both up and down
- Difficulties concentrating
- Stomach cramps, other non-specific gastrointestinal complaints (constipation, acid reflux, etc.)

Health Consequences of Binge Eating Disorder

The health risks of BED are most commonly those associated with clinical obesity, weight stigma, and weight cycling (aka, yo-yo dieting). Most people who are labeled clinically obese do not have binge eating disorder. However, of individuals with BED, up to two-thirds are labelled clinically obese; people who struggle with binge eating disorder tend to be of normal or higher-than-average weight, though BED can be diagnosed at any weight.

Source: **www.nationaleatingdisorders.org**

National Eating Disorders.com is an excellent source for information on the BED (Binge Eating Disorder)

Helping a loved one with bulimia symptoms

If you think a loved one may have symptoms of bulimia, have an open and honest discussion about your concerns. You can't force someone to seek professional care, but you can offer encouragement and support. You can also help find a qualified doctor or mental health professional, make an appointment, and even offer to go along.

Because most people with bulimia are usually normal weight or slightly overweight, it may not be apparent to others that something is wrong.

Red flags that family and friends may notice include:

- Constantly worrying or complaining about being fat
- Having a distorted, excessively negative body image
- Repeatedly eating unusually large quantities of food in one sitting, especially foods the person would normally avoid
- Strict dieting or fasting after binge eating
- Not wanting to eat in public or in front of others
- Going to the bathroom right after eating, during meals, or for long periods of time
- Exercising too much
- Having sores, scars, or calluses on the knuckles or hands
- Having damaged teeth and gums
- Changing weight
- Swelling in the hands and feet
- Facial and cheek swelling from enlarged glands

Causes

The exact cause of bulimia is unknown. Many factors could play a role in the development of eating disorders, including genetics, biology, emotional health, societal expectations and other issues.

Risk factors

Girls and women are more likely to have bulimia than boys and men are. Bulimia often begins in the late teens or early adulthood.

Factors that increase your risk of bulimia may include:

- **Biology.** People with first-degree relatives (siblings, parents, or children) with an eating disorder may be more likely to develop an eating disorder, suggesting a possible genetic link. Being overweight as a child or teen may increase the risk.

- **Psychological and emotional issues.** Psychological and emotional problems, such as depression, anxiety disorders, or substance-use disorders are closely linked with eating disorders. People with bulimia may feel negatively about themselves. In some cases, traumatic events and environmental stress may be contributing factors.

- **Dieting.** People who diet are at higher risk of developing eating disorders. Many people with bulimia severely restrict calories between binge episodes, which may trigger an urge to again binge eat and then purge. Other triggers for binging can include stress, poor body self-image, food, and boredom.

Complications

Bulimia may cause numerous serious and even life-threatening complications. Possible complications include:

- Negative self-esteem and problems with relationships and social functioning

- Dehydration, which can lead to major medical problems, such as kidney failure

- Heart problems, such as an irregular heartbeat or heart failure

- Severe tooth decay and gum disease

- Absent or irregular periods in females

- Digestive problems

- Anxiety, depression, personality disorders or bipolar disorder
- Misuse of alcohol or drugs
- Self-injury, suicidal thoughts or suicide

Diagnosis

If your primary care provider suspects you have bulimia, he or she will typically:

- Talk to you about your eating habits, weight-loss methods and physical symptoms
- Do a physical exam
- Request blood and urine tests
- Request a test that can identify problems with your heart (electrocardiogram)
- Perform a psychological evaluation, including a discussion of your attitude toward your body and weight
- Use the criteria for bulimia listed in the Diagnostic and Statistical Manual of Mental Disorders (DSM-5), published by the American Psychiatric Association

Your primary care provider may also request additional tests to help pinpoint a diagnosis, rule out medical causes for weight changes and check for any related complications.

Treatment

When you have bulimia, you may need several types of treatment, although combining psychotherapy with antidepressants may be the most effective for overcoming the disorder.

Treatment generally involves a team approach that includes you, your family, your primary care provider, a mental health professional and a dietitian experienced in treating eating disorders. You may have a case manager to coordinate your care.

Here's a look at bulimia treatment options and considerations.

Psychotherapy

Psychotherapy, also known as talk therapy or psychological counseling, involves discussing your bulimia and related issues with a mental health professional. Evidence indicates that these types of psychotherapy help improve symptoms of bulimia:

- **Cognitive behavioral therapy** to help you normalize your eating patterns and identify unhealthy, negative beliefs and behaviors and replace them with healthy, positive ones
- **Family-based treatment** to help parents intervene to stop their teenager's unhealthy eating behaviors, to help the teen regain control over his or her eating, and to help the family deal with problems that bulimia can have on the teen's development and the family
- **Interpersonal psychotherapy**, which addresses difficulties in your close relationships, helping to improve your communication and problem-solving skills

Ask your mental health professional which psychotherapy he or she will use and what evidence exists that shows it's beneficial in treating bulimia.

Medications

Antidepressants may help reduce the symptoms of bulimia when used along with psychotherapy. The only antidepressant specifically approved by the Food and Drug Administration to treat bulimia is fluoxetine (Prozac), a type of selective serotonin reuptake inhibitor (SSRI), which may help even if you're not depressed.

Nutrition education

Dietitians can design an eating plan to help you achieve healthy eating habits to avoid hunger and cravings and to provide good nutrition. Eating regularly and not restricting your food intake is important in overcoming bulimia.

Hospitalization

Bulimia can usually be treated outside of the hospital. But if symptoms are severe, with serious health complications, you may need treatment in a hospital. Some eating disorder programs may offer day treatment rather than inpatient hospitalization.

Treatment challenges in bulimia

Although most people with bulimia do recover, some find that symptoms don't go away entirely. Periods of binging and purging may come and go through the years, depending on your life circumstances, such as recurrence during times of high stress.

If you find yourself back in the binge-purge cycle, follow-up sessions with your primary care provider, dietitian and/or mental health professional may help you weather the crisis before your eating disorder spirals out of control again. Learning positive ways to cope, creating healthy relationships and managing stress can help prevent a relapse.

If you've had an eating disorder in the past and you notice your symptoms returning, seek help from your medical team immediately.

Prevention

Although there's no sure way to prevent bulimia, you can steer someone toward healthier behavior or professional treatment before the situation worsens. Here's how you can help:

- Foster and reinforce a healthy body image in your children, no matter what their size or shape. Help them build confidence in ways other than their appearance.
- Have regular, enjoyable family meals.
- Avoid talking about weight at home. Focus instead on having a healthy lifestyle.
- Discourage dieting, especially when it involves unhealthy weight-control behaviors, such as fasting, using weight-loss supplements or laxatives, or self-induced vomiting.
- Talk with your primary care provider. He or she may be in a good position to identify early indicators of an eating disorder and help prevent its development.
- If you notice a relative or friend who seems to have food issues that could lead to or indicate an eating disorder, consider supportively talking to the person about these issues and ask how you can help.

Source: **https://www.mayoclinic.org**

What Is Purging Disorder?

Purging disorder is an eating disorder that is diagnosed when a person purges to influence shape or weight but does not binge.

It can be thought of as bulimia nervosa without the binging. Most writing about the disorder seem to assume that vomiting is the default form of purging, but laxative and diuretic misuse are also common. Many patients also engage in other behaviors to compensate for eating, including excessive exercise and extreme fasting.

Although purging disorder has likely existed for some time, it was first formally recognized by Keel and colleagues in 2005. Purging disorder has been studied far less than bulimia nervosa. Indeed, many patients with purging disorder may have been incorrectly diagnosed as having bulimia nervosa or may not have been diagnosed at all.

Purging disorder is not listed as an official disorder in the Diagnostic and Statistical Manual of Mental Disorders (DSM-5). Instead, it is included as a described condition within the category of other specified feeding and eating disorder (OSFED).

This category includes individuals with clinically significant eating disorders who do not meet criteria for one of the primary eating disorders including anorexia nervosa, bulimia nervosa, or binge eating disorder. Even though it lacks its own official category, purging disorder can be

Not Clearly Defined

Because purging disorder is not well-defined, researchers have not totally agreed on what it comprises. One of the challenges with our current diagnostic system is deciding into which basket a person with a certain group of symptoms should be placed.

For example, driven exercise has more recently been included as a potential purging behavior. Even though exercise is commonly considered a healthy and socially acceptable behavior—in a way that vomiting or laxative use is not—excessive exercise can be a serious problem.

However, it is not yet clear that excessive exercise behavior is by itself sufficient for a diagnosis of purging disorder. One set of researchers believe that it should be. In their recent study, they found that individuals who engage in regular driven exercise (but do not use other methods of purging) have similar psychopathology as those who purge regularly by vomiting or laxative misuse.

Thus, the research is ongoing and as a result, it is unclear exactly how purging disorder will be defined.

Who Gets Purging Disorder?

Purging disorder most commonly emerges in late adolescence and early adulthood. It affects primarily females and people who are classified as normal weight or greater.

Because of the current diagnostic system, which prioritizes the diagnosis of anorexia nervosa, purging disorder specifically cannot be diagnosed in individuals who are underweight. Individuals who are underweight and engage in purging would instead be diagnosed with anorexia nervosa, binge/purge subtype.

As a proportion of those seeking treatment for an eating disorder, research indicates that purging disorder is the presenting problem in five to ten percent of adult patients and 24 to 28 percent of adolescent patients. It might become a more common diagnosis if individuals with excessive exercise get classified as having purging disorder.

How Is Purging Disorder Different from Bulimia Nervosa and Anorexia Nervosa?

By definition, people with purging disorder do not have the episodes of eating unusually large amounts of food that characterize bulimia nervosa (otherwise they would meet criteria for bulimia nervosa). However, they may often feel that they have eaten "too much" when they have actually only eaten a normal amount of food. They may purge after meals. They may experience similar levels of guilt and shame to those who purge after eating large amounts of food.

Research shows that patients who purge but do not binge have severe symptoms that include restrictive eating, a preoccupation with eating disorder thoughts, and body image concerns. A primary difference between purging disorder and bulimia may be that patients with bulimia nervosa report a greater loss of control over food. Some research suggests that purging disorder may be less severe than bulimia nervosa.

Patients with purging disorder often report feelings of gastrointestinal distress after eating and more distress than healthy people and patients with bulimia nervosa. Some patients with purging disorder may feel that their vomiting is automatic.

According to Keel and colleagues (2017), patients with purging disorder "often resemble patients with anorexia nervosa in temperament and interpersonal interactions more than they resemble patients with bulimia nervosa" (p. 191)

Source: **https://www.verywellmind.com**

According to the National Eating Disorder Association (NEDA), around 20 million women and ten million men in the US experience a clinically significant eating disorder at some point in their lives. Bulimia nervosa: a disorder characterized by people eating a lot of food (binging) and then attempting to get rid of the extra calories in unhealthy ways. This can take the form of purging, through self-induced vomiting or the misuse of laxatives, for example.

Binge eating disorder: a condition whereby unusually large amounts of food are frequently consumed, accompanied by a compulsion to do so. Anorexia nervosa: a disorder characterized by a distorted perception of body weight and a significant fear of gaining weight. People with anorexia nervosa often go to extreme measures to lose weight or prevent weight gain.

We need to raise awareness among smaller sociodemographic groups such as seniors who are traditionally not associated with eating disorders.

"People fail to recognize that eating disorders can strike people of any age," said professor Bulik, the founding director of the University of North Carolina center of excellence for eating disorders. "They think that people magically grow out of eating disorders when they leave adolescence. Nothing could be farther from the truth."

Rather than growing out of eating disorders, many people live with these diseases their entire lives, well into retirement.

"One of the main concerns is that eating disorders take a tremendous toll on just about every bodily system," explains professor Cynthia M. Bulik, " in old age, these body systems are less resilient to begin with, just because of the aging process, so eating disorders can erode them more quickly and more seriously."

Eating disorders are often depicted as a disease that only affects teenagers and younger adults. This is not always the case. Eating disorders can affect anyone, especially older adults who have had the disease since their younger years and have never recovered or have had some amount of recovery but have relapsed. It should not be assumed that an eating disorder that began in the early teens will automatically go away as the person gets older. Like any disease, without treatment many people who have had EDs in their early years are still struggling in their later years.

Young people usually seek help looking forward to their future. Older people are embarrassed to seek help or worse yet, have physicians dismiss them and tell them they have outgrown eating disorder!

Source: **https://www.medicalnewstoday.com**
(Feb 2015)

Notes

My Favorite Bible Verses (NIV)

If we live, we live for the Lord; and if we die, we die for the Lord. So, whether we live or die we belong to the Lord.
Romans 14:8

The Lord does not look at the things people look at. People look at the outward appearance, but the Lord looks at the heart.
1 Samuel 16:7

For his anger lasts only a moment, but his favor lasts a lifetime; weeping may stay for the night, but rejoicing comes in the morning.
Psalm 30:5

Therefore we do not lose heart. Though outwardly we are wasting away, yet inwardly we are being renewed day by day.
2 Corinthians 4:16

So Abraham called that place The Lord Will Provide. And to this day it is said, "On the mountain of the Lord, it will be provided."
Genesis 22:14

Let us hold unswervingly to the hope we profess, for he who promised is faithful.
Hebrews 10:23

He has shown you, O mortal, what is good. And what does the Lord require of you? To act justly and to love mercy and to walk humbly with your God.
Micah 6:8

Take delight in the Lord, and he will give you the desires of your heart.
Psalm 37:4

Bring the whole tithe into the storehouse, that there may be food in my house. Test me in this," says the Lord Almighty, "and see if I will not throw open the floodgates of heaven and pour out so much blessing that there will not be room enough to store it.
MALACHI 3:10

Hatred stirs up conflict, but love covers over all wrongs.
PROVERBS 10:12

Are not all angels ministering spirits sent to serve those who will inherit salvation?
HEBREWS 1:14

The Lord is close to the brokenhearted and saves those who are crushed in spirit
PSALM 34:18

Each heart knows its own bitterness, and no one else can share its joy.
PROVERBS 14:10

I love those who love me, and those who seek me find me.
PROVERBS 8:17

The Lord himself goes before you and will be with you; he will never leave you nor forsake you. Do not be afraid; do not be discouraged.
DEUTERONOMY 31:8

Do not be deceived: God cannot be mocked. A man reaps what he sows.
GALATIANS 6:7

The prayer of a righteous person is powerful and effective.
JAMES 5:16

Resources for Help

Overeaters Anonymous:
https://OA.Org – You are NOT alone anymore! Find a meeting.

Weight Watchers
https://www.weightwatchers.com

Bibliography

https://www.Mednewstoday.com (Feb 2015) Hazelden Meditation Series, Food for Thought, Harper & Row, 1985

https://www.Eatingdisorder.com

https://www.Nationaleatingdisorder.comFI

https://www.Mayoclinic.com

https://www.verywellmind.com

About the Author

Kim Wagner Cain was born and raised on Long Island, NY. Having moved to Las Vegas, NV as an adult, she has resided there for 25 years. Before becoming disabled from a neck injury, she worked in the trade show industry for several years. She was called by God to write a book about her lifetime with an eating disorder that she is currently still living with. She is a devout Christian and, being obedient to God, *Forty Years of Food* is the result of this calling. Her ongoing desire to help others with their own food struggles kept her motivated through her two-year journey in completing this book. She is married to Bill Cain and is the mother of two grown children and grandmother to seven grandchildren, the youngest are three-year old twin boys!

Contact me at:

info@fortyyearsoffood.com
Fortyyearsoffood.com
Facebook: Forty years of food.

Coming Soon:

Forty Years of Food Daily Devotions: 365 Daily Inspirations for the Food Addict"For the compulsive overeater, one extra bite is too much and a thousand are not enough. No matter how much we eat, we are never satisfied. The more we eat, the worse we feel. Rather than satisfying us, the one extra, compulsive bite triggers an insatiable craving which drives us to consume enormous quantities of unnecessary food. Sometimes we stuff ourselves until we are exhausted, physically ill, but we are still not satisfied. Since no amount will ever be enough-or only hope is to abstain from the first extra, compulsive bite".

(Food for Thought-Jan 11)

CPSIA information can be obtained
at www.ICGtesting.com
Printed in the USA
LVHW050822011221
704868LV00013B/1483

9 781640 881976